YEAR OF THE

Storms

DEDICATION

This book is dedicated to the men and women of the
Mennonite Disaster Service whose determination, patience
and serenity in aiding victims of disasters is known
worldwide. A portion of the proceeds from the sale of each
book goes to the Kansas unit of MDS.

The book is also dedicated to the families of Lucas Fisher
and Ruth and Harold Voth. Six-year-old Lucas died a few
feet from his mother's arms when the March 13 tornado
struck their home near Burrton. Ruth Voth was killed near
Goessel where the tornado reached its peak in intensity.
Harold Voth died six months later of cancer. Both had been
missionaries for the Mennonite Central Committee.

YEAR OF THE

Storms

THE DESTRUCTIVE KANSAS WEATHER OF 1990

Howard Inglish
Editor

Hearth Publishing
A Division of Multi Business Press
Hillsboro, Kansas

ACKNOWLEDGMENTS

Editorial: Copy editors Cynthia Mines and Sarah Winter played a key role in editing, advising me on style, and in pitching in when their services were needed. Mines also made an important contribution to the black-and-white page layout. Tim Travis and Carol Duerksen also contributed in the copy editing and photograph-caption writing areas, respectively.

The eleven writers who contributed to this book also gave of their time in many other ways, including the collecting of photographs and assisting in the receptions held across the state. They are: Roberta Birk, Carol Duerksen, Merry Hayes, Cynthia Mines, Larry Peirce, Sara Peterson, Tamra Rundell, Cynthia Snider, Jane Vajnar, Julie Vosberg and Judith Weber.

Publishing: Thanks to the many individuals at Multi Business Press, the Hillsboro-based parent company of Hearth Publishing, whose help and craftsmanship was vital to the project's success. Most specifically, I would like to acknowledge these contributions: Joel Klaassen, marketing director, for approaching me with the project, for his overall help, and for his unwavering support; Stan Thiessen, general manager, for proposing the Storms project idea and having the foresight and fortitude to go forward with the project; Judy Boschmann, administrative assistant who supervised the photo identification process and helped in many other ways;

and D. Andrew West, who did the cover design and advised me on many of the interior design elements.

Color separations provided by Edwards Typographic Service Inc., Wichita. Final type was processed at KPN Typographics Inc., Wichita.

The people at Dillons Stores Inc., Hutchinson, gave the project their early support and belief in it, specifically: John Baldwin, Ken Keefer, Terry Ballinger and Donna Fry.

Others whose advice and support I depended on: Irvin Harms, Moundridge, Kansas chairman, Mennonite Disaster Service; Les Anderson, editor of the Ark Valley News, Valley Center, and his staff for some of the original material in the inland hurricane chapter; and the advice and support of friends, specifically, Randy Brown and Carol Skaff. Meteorologist and Pratt businessman Jon Davies provided both encouragement and technical assistance.

Finally, our thanks is extended to the survivors of the storms that swept Kansas this year. Our gratitude goes to them for their cooperation and for convincing all of us involved that this book was the right and appropriate way to conclude a turbulent and traumatic year.

Howard Inglish
Editor

SECOND EDITION
Copyright © 1990 by Multi Business Press

ISBN 0-9627947-0-8
Library of Congress Catolog Number: 90-84588

CONTENTS

FOREWORD

Four months, 11,000 miles and more than a hundred interviews later I am presented with the tasks of writing a foreword about my experience as editor and project coordinator for Year of the Storms, and of letting our readers know a little more about the book.

What I hope to do in this short space is to give the readers some guideposts to look for along the way as they go through the book. One guidepost is that the book is supplemented to a great degree by photographs, more than 300 in fact. In doing the research for this book, I found no other published in the United States that tries to tell the story of the storms and tornadoes with so many pictures and words.

The photos act as a filmstrip across the page, and much of the material in the filmstrip is not included in the book. Our intention is to place readers in the eye of the storm, as if they are in a helicopter hovering above, then landing to witness the damage and how it altered forever the lives of hundreds of Kansas families.

Kansas tornadoes. The phrase conjures up all kinds of images, the most obvious of which I won't go into here. What I have learned in the past four months — which turned into a crash course on tornadoes and other wind storms — is that the power of a tornado is truly awesome. That message I believe comes home clearly in the text and photographs which tell the stories of more than 500 Kansans interviewed for the book. Most were those whose homes and property were severely damaged or destroyed. And the more than 300 photographs in the book bear witness to the riveting descriptions provided in the text.

More than four score tornadoes touched down in Kansas this year. We concentrate on those that occurred on March 13, April 25, May 24, June 7 and June 19. In addition, the book deals extensively with the shear wind storm that we call the inland hurricane — which whipped through six counties with 115-mile-per-hour winds, leaving more property damage in its wake than all the tornadoes combined. The total damage from all tornadoes and storms in Kansas this year is estimated at more than $150 million.

Whether it was the snapping of trees and poles like toothpicks or the documented stories of cars floating in the air, I was constantly surprised by the similarity of the nature of the tornadoes and the inland hurricane, and the similar damage the two very different kinds of storms left behind.

Still, it is the Kansas tornado that is the heart of the book. To tell the story, 11 writers from across the state were assigned specific storms and tornadoes in August. Receptions were held to meet with survivors and to collect photographs. By the end of the process, we had reviewed more than 4,000 photographs, and of those that appear in this book, about 90 percent have never been published before. It was a real pleasure to discover that amateur photographers could take such outstanding photographs.

In traveling the state, I learned a lot about its people, and to my surprise, I found out they are measurably different from those — including me — who lead our lives in Kansas' largest city, Wichita. The people of the Kansas prairie have a deeper, broader faith, a stronger anchor, and they remember some things about friendships that the fast-paced urbanites have forgotten. The people of the plains are more resolute, determined and steady. All of these qualities served these people well as they faced the tragedy of the incredible devastation that nature wreaked on our state this year.

It's hard to imagine facing the heartache that the families of Ruth and Harold Voth and Lucas Fisher endured this year. And it is to them this book is dedicated. Six-year-old Lucas died a few feet from his mother's arms in their home near Burrton, and Ruth Voth was killed near Goessel where the March 13 tornado reached its peak in intensity. Harold Voth died six months later of cancer.

The Voth home and farm were demolished as if tons of explosives had been set loose. The tornado, packing winds in excess of 300 miles per hour, left the farm looking like a war zone, with home and outbuildings and cars and farm equipment stirred together as if a giant egg beater had processed it all, leaving behind only a barely recognizable scene.

One of the other sad stories a tornado brings is the death to livestock. There was more than $20 million in damages to farm and livestock from the storms of 1990. Out in the open and exposed to penetrating debris, they do not die a pleasant death.

Often a tornado striking a house or farm was not the first misfortune for a family: Some battled illness, some had battled other major storms only a few months earlier. This double and sometimes triple whammy was felt particularly in Reno County, which was hit with five major storms in a three-month period.

A poignant example of a multiple tragedy occurred in Marion County, which was the ending point for both the March 13 and May 24 tornadoes. Ernest and Agnes Bina's farm was hit on March 13. On May 24 and only a few miles away, the farm owned by their son and daughter-in-law, Dean and Pat Bina, was struck by a tornado. On June 13 Ernest Bina died of cancer.

Of course, the good news and the true miracle of the storms of 1990 is that more people didn't die.

There were only two fatalities from all the tornadoes, and neither of those was within the city limits of Hesston where the tornado left such devastation. The people of Hesston, a strongly Mennonite community in south central Kansas just off I-135, were wise enough to seek appropriate shelter.

I do understand the fascination many have with tornadoes.

The menacing dark cloud and funnel leaves people in awe, too dumbstruck to move at times, as the twister marches across the open prairie with death and destruction draped around its jagged edges.

The more pleasant note that the book ends on is that the people of Hesston have bounced back. To drive through that city today and view its gleaming new homes and businesses leaves little hint of the amazing destruction that occurred. A war zone is an accurate description for that city, too, on the evening of March 13.

It was on the evening of March 13 that the first few hundred of what would later grow to be thousands of volunteers converged on that town. And making up the largest portions of that volunteer corps were members of Mennonite Disaster Service. The 1990 tornadoes struck in the heart of Kansas Mennonite country, which meant that many of those on the receiving end of assistance had in other disasters been on the scene to provide assistance as MDS volunteers.

The story we heard time and time again from the storm survivors was their marvel at the dedication of the men and women of the Mennonite Disaster Service to whom this book is also dedicated. A typical response from a survivor: "People we didn't even know came from miles away, sometimes hundreds of miles away, and stayed for days to help. Why do they do it?"

We try to answer that and many other questions in this book. But my version of the answer is that with patience, serenity, and determination, the people of MDS go about mending fences and lives.

Howard Inglish
November 1990

The May 24 tornado is increasing in size as it nears Holyrood. In the first photo, the tornado's width is estimated to be between three-quarters and a mile wide. In the second photo, the tornado is seen from a mile and a half away. Photos from the video by Allen Hurley furnished by Jon Davies.

The Weather of 1990: What a Year!

The late 1980s brought fame and fortune to Kansas via its winning sports teams — the University of Kansas Jayhawks with the coveted NCAA basketball championship and the Wichita State University Shockers with their number one spot in the college baseball series. Kansas, however, began the 1990s by breaking weather records instead. As Jack May, Kansas area manager for the National Weather Service in Topeka, observed, "We've returned to normal and then some."

And many people's thoughts were echoed on T-shirts sold to commemorate the March 13 tornado: "Gee, Toto, I think we're back in Kansas."

It was a year that Kansans won't soon forget: The weather roller-coaster started in March, with 22 tornadoes recorded through March 13. The first sighting of the year was in western Reno County March 11. A small tornado formed from a thunderstorm with a top of only 23,000 feet. Fifteen minutes later, a tornado touched down in Rice County.

The next day, Monday, March 12, brought 17 reports of hail and windstorms, mostly confined to the northeastern counties. In fact, the first tornado of March 13 occurred a few minutes after midnight at McLouth, about 40 miles west of Kansas City. The twister had first touched down about 11:45 p.m. on March 12 in Topeka. In Wichita, a representative from Sedgwick County's disaster management department met with KWCH-TV staff to update the television station's emergency preparedness plan. In Newton, ham radio operator Gary Boldenow installed a new antenna cable

at the Harvey County Courthouse communications center. No doubt, other timely scenes were played out in a prelude to the major devastation that was to occur the following day.

Tuesday, March 13, started out like any other day for most of central Kansas. By 9 a.m., the daily round of school, work, meetings and appointments had begun. About 30 minutes later, an unusual early-morning tornado watch was issued for much of central Kansas, in effect from 10 a.m. to 4 p.m. That afternoon, the watch was extended to 10 p.m.

The first tornado sighting of the afternoon came at 4:34 p.m. when a tornado touched down two miles northeast of Pretty Prairie in southern Reno County, moving northeast at a rapid 40 miles per hour.

The tornado sped from the Pretty Prairie area to an area between Yoder and Haven, damaging houses and power lines. Weather watchers initially feared the twister would strike Haven, but it passed north of the city. At approximately 5 p.m., the tornado struck the Burrton area. A six-year-old boy was killed when a chimney collapsed in the basement of his rural home.

At 5:30 p.m. the tornado plowed into Hesston cutting a terrible swath across the city and injuring at least 13 people. Forty to 50 percent of the town received damage. Almost 300 were left homeless within a 15-minute period, but miraculously no one in Hesston died. Later the tornado claimed the life of an elderly Goessel woman.

According to meteorologist Jon Davies, the Hesston tornado outbreak included at least four separate tor-

Tornado Chasers

Meteorologist and Pratt businessman Jon Davies is successful enough in his medical supply business that he has time to pursue the avocation that is close to his heart: chasing tornadoes whenever skies look threatening. Davies followed the south central Kansas March 13 tornado from its birth near Pretty Prairie to the Burrton area, where power lines blocked his way. Another tornado-chaser, whose car received a solid pounding from the March 13 tornado, is Doug Nelson, who makes his living as a carpenter in the Alma area.

On March 13, Nelson rushed to west of Hesston when he heard reports a tornado had touched down in Reno County headed northeast. His color photos are some of the most dramatic of the storm. "I tried to stay ahead of it, but I chickened out and parked underneath the overpass." he said. "I saw pieces of roof flying by." Nelson continued to follow the tornado toward Hillsboro, capturing it at its intensity as it crossed K-15. At some points he was within a half-mile of the funnel. He followed it until dark near Dwight. "It almost got me there. It was so dark," he said.

Nelson, like Davies, has been trained as a spotter through the National Weather Service. "The public and the media shouldn't follow them as closely as I do. One of these days, someone who doesn't know what they're doing is going to get killed."

Far Right: North of Haven, the March 13 tornado has been on the ground about half an hour as it races toward Burrton. Photo by Robert Williams.

Jon Davies

nadoes. The first tornado, which began near Pretty Prairie, was rated F4 at Hesston, where it narrowed to a path of 200 yards wide. The F4 rating is applied to a devastating tornado of 207-260 miles per hour on an intensity scale (0 to 5) developed by Dr. Theodore Fujita, widely recognized as a leading tornado expert.

The second tornado touched down just northeast of Hesston and paralleled the first tornado for two miles until they converged at approximately 5:45 p.m., forming a larger tornado that grew rapidly to F5 intensity (261-318 mph). Whether the F5 was a third tornado or just an enhancement of the second tornado is open to question, said Davies. The F5 tornado followed a path south of Goessel to just east of Goessel, where the deadly storm claimed its second fatality of the day, a 65-year-old woman found near her farm home. The F5 tornado finally lifted just shy of Marion Reservoir east of Hillsboro around 6:15 p.m.

Another tornado occurred just east of Pilsen at 6:30 p.m. and continued into the Flint Hills to north of Alta Vista at 7:35 p.m. Its strongest intensity was rated F2 (113-157 mph) near Delavan. The last of the Hesston tornado gang touched down briefly about six miles northeast of Wamego at 8:03 p.m. with an F1 (73-112 mph) intensity.

March 13 was a record-breaking day for Kansas tornadoes. Consider:

- Meteorologist Jon Davies mapped 17 tornadoes occurring in Kansas March 13 between 4:30 p.m. and 10 p.m. The last major tornado in Kan-

sas touched down just before 7 p.m. north of Burrton and took an unusual northerly path toward McPherson. The funnel caused more than $1 million damage to 20 homes. Davies' mapping also showed 40 other tornadoes during that time in Texas, Oklahoma, Nebraska, Missouri and Iowa.

- A typical Kansas tornado stays on the ground for about 10 minutes, but the storm that ravaged Hesston was on the ground for two-and-a-half hours as it crossed much of central Kansas.

- Average speed of a tornado is between 30 and 35 mph. The Hesston tornadoes were reported moving at 40 mph.

- The average length a tornado stays on the ground is six miles. The Hesston tornadoes traveled over 100 miles. According to preliminary research by the National Weather Service in Topeka, the Salina tornado of 1973 was the last time a tornado crossed more than 100 miles in Kansas.

- At several points along its path, the major March 13 tornado was estimated to be at least three-quarters of a mile wide.

- The two March 13 tornado deaths are the earliest tornado-related deaths for any year on record in Kansas. The previous record for earliest deaths was March 15. The two fatalities were also the first tornado-related deaths in

Marvin Hatch of Sedgwick shot this photograph of a twister that touched down in Harvey County about 7 p.m. April 9. The tornado is three-and-a-half miles north of Sedgwick on the Sedgwick-Harvey county line. At this point, the twister is about one quarter mile wide and Hatch reported he could hear the classic "freight train" roar. The tornado damaged the farm of C. G. McGuinn, but the home of Dave and Denise Manning, seen in the foreground at left, was not damaged.

Kansas since 1984.

- The Hesston F4 and F5 tornadoes comprise a category that is less than 2 percent of all tornadoes. During the 1980s, only three of this intensity occurred over the entire country. The last F4 recorded in the state was May 10, 1985, in north central Kansas.

- The Hesston outbreak could rank as high as second in terms of the number of tornadoes spawned by a late winter/early spring storm.

- Meteorologist Mike Smith of WeatherData Inc. said the F5 Hesston tornado may be the most intense tornado ever recorded.

But the Hesston tornadoes weren't the only violent storms recorded in Kansas during 1990.

- On April 25, four tornadoes in sequence from one thunderstorm swept across Ellis County in western Kansas during a four- to five-hour period. The strongest was recorded with an F3 intensity. Total paths on the ground were nearly 120 miles, about the same as the Hesston tornadoes. Fortunately, the tornadoes struck mostly in open country, but estimated damage was still over $1 million.

- On May 24, four or more tornadoes occurred northeast of Great Bend near Claflin, Holyrood, Bushton and Lorraine. The tornadoes formed from at least two and possibly three different thunderstorms during a three-hour time period. The total tornado paths were close to 100 miles long. An F4 tornado that narrowly missed Lorraine by one-fourth mile blew 88 cars of a 125-car train off the track between Claflin and Bushton. Total damage from the storms was nearly $6 million.

- On June 7, at least nine tornadoes developed from several thunderstorms in east central and northeast Kansas, with the most intense recorded at the western edge of Emporia with an F2 rating. All the tornadoes were 100 yards wide or less with path lengths of 10 miles or less. Seventeen injuries were reported in Emporia and the city's damage was estimated at $26 million. The last tornado of the evening occurred about 11 p.m. near Pretty Prairie — not far from where the Hesston tornado had begun three months earlier. The twister, which caused no major damage, moved from southeast to northwest, a very unusual movement for tornadoes, Davies said. Most tornadoes move southwest to northeast or south to north, he said.

- On June 19, a rare and unusually violent hurricane-strength wind storm blasted south central Kansas causing millions of dollars worth of property damage, massive utility outages, gas leaks and numerous injuries. Kansas held on through the night as three waves of rowdy

After decimating farms in the Goessel area, the March 13 tornado is shown in the photo about three miles south of Hillsboro, and is headed for Old Highway 56. Photo furnished by Curt and Jason Vajnar.

Right: The Royer home north of Haven is surrounded by trees maintaining their lonely vigil after being stripped of life by the March 13 tornado. Photo by Eric Stites.

Above: Kurt Lawrence took this photograph facing southwest from his basement window, a mile north and three-and-a-half miles east of Goessel.

storms carrying a menagerie of thunderstorms, tornadoes, hail and 100 to 120 mile-per-hour winds roared through cities, townships and farmsteads. The first rumbled from Pratt to El Dorado from about 9 p.m. to 10:30 p.m., knocking many Wichita television and radio stations off the air at 9:45 p.m. A second wave again battered Sedgwick County and its neighbors from about 12:30 a.m. until 1:30 a.m. And another slashed through Grant County shortly before midnight. Meteorologists called the series of wind shear storms one of the worst of the past century.

Tornado season in Kansas traditionally falls in April, May and June. For the past 40 years, the average number of tornadoes per year in Kansas has been 42. In 1988 and 1989, the number of tornadoes was below average, 24 and 31, respectively — but then came 1990.

It was a record-breaking year for severe weather reports — from the number and intensity of tornadoes and thunderstorms to the millions of dollars in damages caused by destructive windstorms and flash floods. Through June, the National Weather Service's computer printouts listed 85 tornado sightings in Kansas, more than double the average. And late August temperatures careened toward 110 degrees as the days boiled in a runaway heat wave, much like the June heat wave that forced Wichita and other Kansas cities to institute water rationing.

When it comes to explaining Mother Nature, some meteorologists have their theories, some offer educated guesses, and others say they just don't know.

Mike Smith, president of WeatherData Inc., a private weather forecasting firm in Wichita, said he has continued to extrapolate the 45-year cycle of severe weather activity that was first researched by tornado expert Dr. Theodore Fujita of the University of Chicago. According to Smith, "The decade of the '90s as far as tornadoes in Kansas are concerned is going to be much more like the decade of the '50s than it was in the '70s and '80s, many years of which had below normal numbers of tornadoes in the central plains."

The worst recorded tornado in number of lives lost in Kansas was the killer twister that destroyed the small town of Udall in northeast Cowley County, killing 80 and injuring 270 on May 25, 1955. Until 1990, that was also the year for the highest number of recorded tornadoes in Kansas — 98. The worst year in Kansas for tornado property damage was 1966, with almost half a billion dollars spent in repairs and rebuilding in the Topeka area.

Fujita's original paper on the cycle theory was published in 1975, said Smith. It suggested that tornado activity may rotate clockwise throughout the country, with particular areas experiencing strong tornado outbreaks for six to seven years. Fujita, however, in an interview five months after the March 13 Hesston tornado, said he had not continued to research his cycle theory and had questions of its applicability. The cycles not withstanding, Fujita said initial data does in-

Triple vortices in the tornado can be seen as it rolls across Hesston in this Dean Alison video. When a tornado gives birth to multiple vortices, they are contained within the overall funnel. These vortices can punish one house but leave the rest of the tornadic winds to do damage to another.

Looking into the eye of a tornado

One of the best eyewitness descriptions ever recorded of a close up view of a tornado was reported 60 years ago. The description is by a Greensburg, Kansas, farmer Will Keller, who related his story of what happened on the afternoon of June 22, 1928, to a weather bureau official. The report appeared in the Monthly Weather Review, May 1930, published by the U.S. Weather Bureau.

Mr. Keller survived unharmed, but he did the very foolish thing of not following his family down into the cellar. A cloud with three tornadoes hung overhead. His story: "Everything was still as death. There was a strong gassy odor, and I could hardly breathe. There was a screaming hissing sound coming directly from the end of the funnel. I looked up and to my astonishment, I saw right into the heart of the tornado. There was a circular opening in the center of the funnel, about fifty or a hundred feet in diameter and extending straight upwards for a distance of at least a half mile, as best I could judge under the circumstances. The walls of this opening were rotating clouds and the hole was brilliantly lighted with the constant flashes of lightning which zigzagged from side to side. Had it not been for the lightning, I could not have seen the opening or any distance into it.

"Around the rim of the great vortex, small tornadoes were constantly forming and breaking away. These looked like tails as they writhed their way around the funnel. It was these that made the hissing sound. I noticed the rotation of the great whirl was anti-clockwise, but some of the small twisters rotated clockwise. The opening was entirely hollow. I had plenty of time to get a good view of the whole thing, inside and out."

dicate the Hesston tornado was one of the most powerful ever recorded. Fujita said he would release the final conclusion on the Hesston tornado in 1991.

In late October, the National Weather Service — after further study of damage data — was considering upgrading the Hesston tornado's strength within the city limits of Hesston to an F5 status, Davies said.

Davies, a former television meteorologist for the Atlanta 9 weather channel and a Pratt businessman, did his own mapping of the March 13 tornado outbreak. In addition to Davies and Smith, other Kansas meteorologists and weather watchers have submitted data, photos and video footage on the Hesston tornadoes to Fujita.

As for the continued debate over severe weather cycles, there's a lot of research on both sides, says veteran meteorologist Jim O'Donnell of Wichita's KAKE-TV. As he puts it, "Cycles are cycles, but Mother Nature does what she very well pleases. This thing has changed so rapidly. This summer, we went from an extremely hot and dry period to a very wet period to another hot period where we had 105-plus degrees for 11 days and then bam! we're all of a sudden back down in the 80s for a while and then back up to 110 at the end of August. So we try to develop a pattern for that, and I think God's trying to tell us something. Like, 'Remember all those forecasts you set up? They won't work. Try again.' "

National Weather Service area manager Jack May said he, too, had no theories about the unpredictable weather in the Kansas area in 1990. "It's very difficult to predict patterns and we don't put much credibility

into long-range forecasts," he said.

For those who do like to have at least some type of hypothesis on which to peg a changing weather scene, there are several that have been written about. In addition to the popular theory that weather tends to follow cycles, there are others to consider, including sun spots, solar activity which fluctuates over 11-year and 22-year cycles; El Nino, a sharp increase in ocean temperatures in the South Pacific off the coast of Chile that correlates to the way the jet stream moves, and the greenhouse effect.

"Kansas is an interesting state for weather simply because of the way we're set up in the nation," said meteorologist John Ridge. "The Rockies are to the west, the Gulf is to the south, Canada air from the north — we're right in the middle of everything, so anything can and does happen."

The principal villain in 1990, meteorologists said, was a persistent pattern in the upper atmosphere that included low pressure over the West Coast. That in turn routed the jet stream to an unusually low latitude across northwest Mexico and then northeast across the Plains and the Ohio Valley.

"It's like a river of air," said Fred Ostby of the National Severe Storms Forecast Center in Kansas City, "drawing warm, moist air from the Gulf and causing a lot of episodes of severe weather and flooding. Meanwhile, there has been a tendency for that pattern to continually re-establish itself."

Through the first six months of 1990, the nation

Tornado Facts
You Should Know

- Tornadoes can occur any place in the United States at any time of the year. They happen most frequently in the midwestern, southern and central states from March through September.

- Tornado weather can be hot, sticky days with southerly winds and a threatening, ominous sky. Familiar thunderstorm clouds are present. An hour or two before a tornado, topsy-turvy clouds appear sometimes bulging down instead of up. The clouds often have a greenish-black color. Rain, frequently hail, precede the tornado with a heavy downpour after it has passed.

- Tornadoes occur mostly between 3 and 7 p.m., but they have occurred at all hours.

- Tornadoes in most cases move from a westerly direction, usually from the southwest. The tornado's path is usually 10 to 40 miles (the average length is 16 miles), but they may move forward for 300 miles. The average width of the path is about 400 yards, but they have cut swaths more than one mile wide.

- Tornadoes travel about 25 to 40 miles per hour, with wind speed estimated as high as 300 miles per hour within the tornado.

- Tornadoes cause destruction with violent winds which uproot trees, destroy buildings, and create a serious hazard by blowing objects through the air, and by differences in air pressure which can cause buildings to collapse.

National Weather Service

had seen about 800 tornadoes, a figure exceeded only twice since 1950. In Kansas, the number of tornadoes recorded through September 10 was 127. This is a preliminary figure, said Ed Ferguson, also of the National Severe Storms Center in Kansas City. That number will probably shrink about 20 percent after duplicate reports are eliminated, Ferguson said.

With the Hesston tornado, the weather conditions on March 13 represented a classic case for tornado set-up, said KWCH-TV meteorologist Merril Teller.

"That day we had very warm temperatures, plenty of humidity and a good jet stream coming across the area. As I recall, we had southerly winds near the surface, but the jet stream aloft was more west to southwesterly. One of the things you look for in the development of severe weather and tornadoes is wind shear — varying directions of wind in the different levels of the atmosphere — and we had that.

"Once the thunderstorm developed in Reno County, it was just an isolated thunderstorm and it had the advantage of being able to draw in air from all around without other storms taking away from it. So a lot of moisture got to feed into that storm. And it had a clear track. There were clear skies everywhere. It was the first of the thunderstorms that developed that day. Everything came together — the moisture, the heat, the wind shear — just north of Pretty Prairie. That's where the tornado also started.

"Tornadoes develop in the developing part of the thunderstorms where the air is rising a lot. The most likely place for a tornado to develop is on the tail end

'*We provided the communications from Hesston to the outside world.*'
— Gary Boldenow

of the line where there's new development of thunderstorms on the south end." That's what happened with the Hesston tornado, Teller said.

Lon Buller, emergency preparedness coordinator for Harvey County, had his hands full March 13 when the F4-F5 tornadoes swirled through the north end of his county. But he was prepared. And he, along with volunteer spotters and ham radio operators, helped prepare the rest of the county — in particular, Hesston.

"We set sirens off three different times in Hesston," Buller said. "The sirens and warnings and radio and TV helped save people. My advice is always be prepared. Most any community would be able to handle something like this as long as they do the preparation. You need to have a plan and to exercise that plan."

Gary Boldenow said he is one of about 40 ham radio operators in the Newton and Harvey County area. "We've never really had a formal plan because we never know where we're going to be," he said. The hams, as they're often called, were busy just about all night long on March 13. "Primarily, we provided the communications from Hesston to the outside world," Boldenow said. "They were without electricity, the phone service was nil and the emergency people didn't have radios they could really talk to each other with. Police could talk to police but not to firemen or rescue people."

The ham radio operators started their work about 20 minutes after the tornado struck Hesston. "We did a little bit of everything," Boldenow said. "We ordered generators, food and porta-potties. You name it, and I

6

Large chunks of buildings are lifted into the tornado's funnel as its roars across Hesston with internal wind speeds approaching 300 miles per hour. Photo from the Dean Alison video.

Facts That Can Save Your Life

Tornado Awareness

TORNADO WATCH: Issued when the atmosphere is favorable for development of tornadoes. Listen and be prepared to act quickly.

TORNADO WARNING: A tornado has been sighted in the area or indicated on radar. Take cover! Listen to your radio or television for more weather information.

Safety Procedures

AT WORK:
1. Stay away from windows.
2. Avoid areas with large, poorly supported roofs.
3. Take shelter in the basement or inner hallway on a lower level or other predetermined safety area.

AT HOME:
1. Stay away from windows.
2. Take shelter in your basement, preferably under heavy furniture.
3. If you have no basement, take cover under heavy furniture on the ground floor in the center part of the house or small room on the ground floor away from outside walls and windows.
4. If time permits, shut electricity and fuel lines off. Open doors and windows on opposite side of approaching storm. Do not remain in a trailer, mobile home or vehicle.

AT SCHOOL:
1. Stay away from windows.
2. Avoid auditoriums and gymnasiums.
3. If school is of reinforced construction stay inside, near inside wall on the lower floor.

IN OPEN COUNTRY:
1. Move at right angles to tornado's path.
2. If there is no time to escape, lie flat in nearest ditch, ravine, culvert, or under bridge. Do not stay in your car.

Source: Kansas Division of Emergency Preparedness.

think it was done. We were the ones who called other highway patrolmen. And when the governor showed up, we did a couple of telephone patches for him."

The ham operators also figured they handled around 450 to 500 messages over a three-day period, helping relieve a much overburdened telephone system.

As life returned to some sense of normalcy over the next few weeks, emergency preparedness coordinator Buller said he was contacted by various facilities to conduct training sessions. "I've gotten a lot of calls from businesses asking, 'Where do we put our employees or our customers if we go into a tornado warning?' "

Pat Glynn, a disaster management officer for Sedgwick County, said he also was busy. "We've given many more speeches and contacted many more people this year. I think the awareness level has jumped up simply because we've had so many tornadoes this year. We're available literally 24 hours a day. I've given speeches as early as 6:30 a.m. and as late as 11:30 at night — in school halls, conference rooms, taverns. We don't care how many people are there — one or a thousand. If we save the life of one person, it was worth it."

The loss of two lives in the Hesston tornado was tragic, but it could have been much worse, weather observers said. "There's a much better awareness these days," said Jack May of the National Weather Service in Topeka. "Over the years, we've put a tremendous amount of tornado education in the schools. Those people are growing up, moving into society and they're

able to take care of themselves and their parents. They know what to do. Our focus on tornado awareness is paying off."

"Whenever I talk to groups, I always tell them that tornadoes can happen any time and it only takes one," said Teller. "We were fortunate that we went through about three years when there was very little severe weather in Kansas. Now look at the turnaround in 1990. Any given year could go either way. You always have to be ready." □

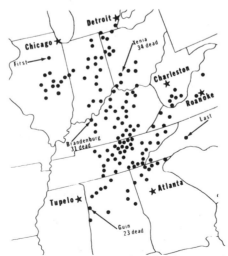

The nation's largest tornado outbreak was on April 3 and 4, 1974 between midnight and 7 a.m. One hundred and forty-eight tornadoes caused 315 deaths and more than $600 million in property damage over an 11 state area. Source: National Weather Service.

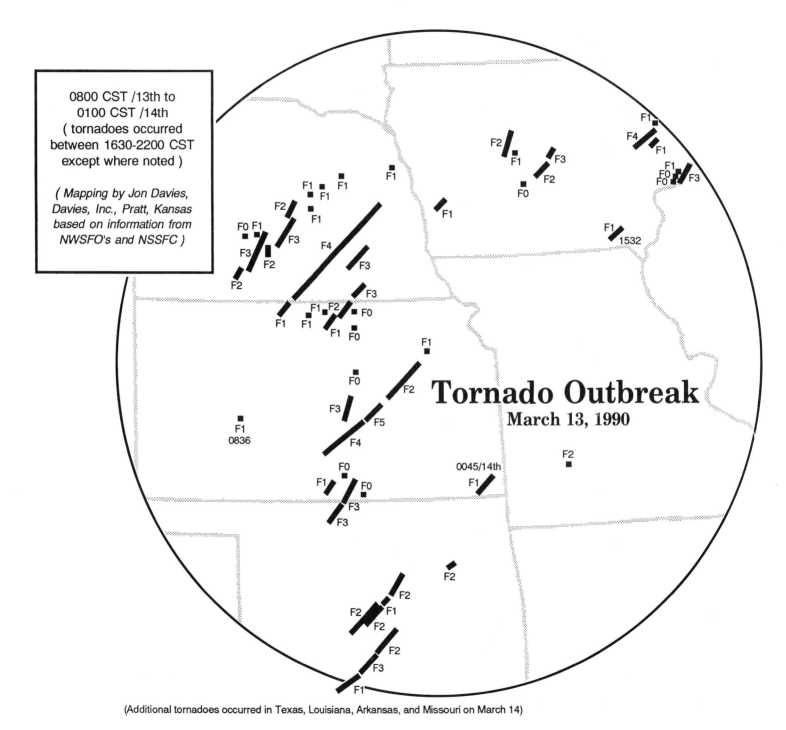

0800 CST /13th to
0100 CST /14th
(tornadoes occurred
between 1630-2200 CST
except where noted)

(*Mapping by Jon Davies,*
Davies, Inc., Pratt, Kansas
based on information from
NWSFO's and NSSFC)

F2
F1
F3
F2

F1

F4
F1
F1

F1
F0
F0
F3

F1
F1
F1

F1

F0
F1
F3
F2
F1
F3

F2

F1
F2
F1
F3
F4

F3

F1
F1
F2
F0
F1
F0
F0
F3

F1
1532

F1

F0

F1
0836

Tornado Outbreak
March 13, 1990

F2
F2
F5
F4

F2

F1
F0
F0
F3
F3

0045/14th
F1

F2

F2

F2
F2
F1
F2

F2
F3
F1

(Additional tornadoes occurred in Texas, Louisiana, Arkansas, and Missouri on March 14)

8

Dick and Margaret Dwyer survey the remains of their home, which took them 12 years to build at the Hutchinson Water Sports Club near Burrton. One of the Dwyers' boats was found in a tree; a sailboat and dock they made were never found. Photo by Sandra J. Watts of The Hutchinson News.

The March 13 Tornadoes:
The First Hour of Terror Before Hesston

BULLETIN —
IMMEDIATE BROADCAST REQUESTED
SEVERE THUNDERSTORM WARNING
NATIONAL WEATHER SERVICE WICHITA KS
420 PM CST TUE MAR 13 1990

THE NATIONAL WEATHER SERVICE HAS ISSUED
A SEVERE THUNDERSTORM WARNING EFFECTIVE
UNTIL 515 PM CST IN THE FOLLOWING COUNTY

IN THE SOUTH CENTRAL PART OF KANSAS

RENO

AT 318 PM A SEVERE THUNDERSTORM WAS IN
THE RENO COUNTY AREA. THIS THUNDERSTORM
IS PRODUCING GOLF BALL SIZED HAIL AND IS
MOVING NORTHEAST AT 40 MPH. IT IS LOCATED
NEAR PRETTY PRAIRIE OR JUST NORTH OF THE
KINGMAN COUNTY LINE.

REMEMBER . . . SEVERE THUNDERSTORMS CAN
AND OCCASIONALLY DO PRODUCE TORNADOES
WITH LITTLE OR NO ADVANCE WARNING. BE ON
THE LOOKOUT.

Storm watches and warnings are not unusual in Kansas during the spring and summer months. Bill Rogers, who lives three miles north and three west of Pretty Prairie, had heard them many times before. On March 13, when he heard of the severe thunderstorm about 20 miles to the south near Kingman, he wasn't overly concerned. He did park the vehicles inside the shed before he settled down inside to read the mail and watch television.

"At 4:35 the electricity went off, so I decided to get up and look out the window," Bill recalled. "There was a tornado about one quarter mile away from the house, coming right towards me. I didn't really know what to do. We have an outside cellar, but I didn't think I had time to get there. So I did what I'd always told Matt (Bill's step-son) to do — go to the inside hallway of the house. I remember seeing limbs fly by as I looked out the window, and the horse running like crazy. It was over real quick. I got up and went to look, expecting to see a lot of damage. But I didn't expect stuff to actually be gone!"

Gone were a large machine shed, barn, grain bins and outbuildings. Huge trees were either uprooted or twisted and torn. The house suffered roof damage and broken windows and was infiltrated with dirt, glass, grass and sticks.

Less than three miles northeast of Bill Rogers' farm, 72-year-old Eileen Berndsen was dusting her living room. She turned on the TV, heard a tornado was heading northeast from Pretty Prairie, and looked out her front door.

The tornado originated near Pretty Prairie and headed northeast toward Hesston, narrowly missing Haven, Yoder and Burrton.

Bill Rogers, who lives three miles north and three west of Pretty Prairie, stands next to a large tree uprooted by the twister. Photo by Carol Duerksen.

One of the first farm homes to be hit by the tornado was the Mike Astle residence, located three miles south of Yoder on the Arlington-Haven Road. Photo by Don Fischer.

"I saw the wall, and I knew it was the real thing because I could see it rotating on the sides. So I closed the door and went to the basement. I was going to look out the southwest corner of the basement, but about that time the windows blew out."

Eileen's 76-year-old husband Henry Berndsen, enroute from Hutchinson, was less than a mile from home when he saw the quarter-mile wide funnel sweep his farm. He knew his wife was there alone.

He drove into the yard to see all seven of his farm buildings destroyed. Farm equipment, vehicles and trees lay twisted and mangled. Only the house remained, and from it emerged Eileen, uninjured.

After seeing his wife was okay, Berndsen's first words were, "We don't have a car to drive."

"They were in the garage," Eileen told him.

"We don't have a garage," he said.

Seven miles to the northeast, Caroline Haines abandoned her truck and took refuge in a ditch three miles south of Yoder. She had been on her way home from the Agricultural, Stabilization and Conservation Service office in South Hutchinson.

"I live three miles from Yoder, and my pickup started rocking and it was hailing. I figured I'd better get out and lay in the ditch. That's when I saw the tornado about a half mile away. I saw two tails come out, and it hit my neighbor Mick Astle's house. At first I thought it was his garbage blowing around, but it was pieces of the house. I also saw it pulling trees straight up into the air."

Caroline was uninjured and returned home to find damage to her house, outbuildings, and the water sucked out of the swimming pool. Her neighbors, Mick and Edna Astle, both 74, had been lying in an interior hallway of their house when the storm hit. When it was over, that hallway was the only part of the home that still had a ceiling, and they were safe.

At 4:25 p.m., 63-year-old Polly Fry stepped out on the back porch of her farm home three miles southeast of Yoder. She noticed the big dark cloud in the southwest but decided to go about her evening chores letting the chickens out and gathering and washing the eggs. Then she heard the Haven siren go off.

Polly grabbed a flashlight, stopped to let the dog into the back porch, and saw the big black cloud about one-quarter mile away.

"It sounded like a freight train, and stuff was boiling around in it," she remembered. "I was going to get in the southwest corner of the basement, but I didn't want the shelves of canned fruit to fall on me, so I just sat on the bottom stair step.

"I felt like my head was going to explode, and I can't describe the sound. It was just awful! I prayed, 'If you want to take everything else, just save my life.' I heard a pop — and then it got so dusty I could hardly breathe. I think that's probably when the house was lifted and set back down."

Sometimes, Polly said, when she closes her eyes, she can still see and hear what happened in those few minutes during and after the tornado's passing. Farm buildings, machinery, vehicles and trees were thrown together and bent grotesquely. The Fry homestead,

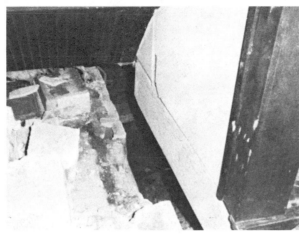

LEFT: Dean Eales recalls his close encounter with the twister: "This tornado never made any attempt to raise or get off the ground. . . . It was ungodly." Photo by Carol Duerksen.

RIGHT: Eighty-three-year-old John Devenpeck squeezed through a space of less than 10 inches to escape his basement. Photo by Boneva Hammar.

once filled with hedge, cedar and shade trees, was virtually unrecognizable.

In a state of shock and disbelief, Polly began walking to her neighbors'. She was picked up by Dean Eales, a Yoder Fire Department volunteer and weather watcher who was tracking the storm. Moments later they met her husband Floyd coming home from his job at Yoder Hardware.

"We lost everything! We lost everything!" Polly cried repeatedly. Floyd Fry saw it differently.

"I still have you," he said.

Dean Eales had seen many tornadoes over the years, but none that were as large or that stayed on the ground as long as this one.

"Most generally, they'll go a mile or so, raise up, and then go down again," he said. "But this one never made any attempt to raise or get off the ground. It looked like it was a shy half-mile wide. It was ungodly."

Eales watched the tornado from a quarter mile away and said the noise in his pickup was so bad he couldn't talk on the radio.

Eales watched as a shiny stock tank rode the whirlwind up and down, up and down, up and down. Eales estimated he saw it about 200 yards up inside the tornado, then near the ground, then at the top again, for at least three cycles. "In that black cloud, the tank really stuck out," he said.

While the truck shook and the body suffered hail damage and sand blasting, the tornado deposited debris in the pickup bed.

"I found old barn boards and tree limbs back there when I got home that night," he said. "The windows weren't cracked and there weren't other dents in the truck, but it had dumped this stuff in the pickup bed."

About a mile from the Fry farmstead, the home of Bill and Leta Royer stood directly in the twister's path. Unaware of the approaching storm, they were watching a video when the electricity clicked off and then back on. As Leta got up to start the VCR again, she looked out the window and saw the wall cloud.

"I've always thought if I could see a tornado, I'd outrun it," Royer recalled, "so we left, and watched it from two miles south of our place."

When they returned, the Royers were shocked to see the difference the tornado had made in a matter of seconds. Their huge old landmark barn was a pile of rubble. Other outbuildings, vehicles and trees were destroyed. The farmhouse remained, but was trashed throughout. Their son, Bill Jr., had arrived home moments before the tornado hit and had ridden it out safely in the basement.

Tony and Connie Brauer, who live about one-and-a-half miles northeast of the Royers, also drove away from the impending disaster. Like the Royers, the Brauers were met with destruction when they returned home.

"The brick walls of the house were there, but they were sucked in," Brauer said. "Inside, it was a total mess. We also lost an outbuilding, deck and pasture fences."

A half mile to the east was a scene that hurt Brauer almost more than the destruction of his home — the

Deciding whether or not to rebuild on their land was a tough decision for Polly and Floyd Fry. Says Polly: "We're at the age where we're too young to retire, but starting over is so hard."

The Kent and Dixie Fisher family are seen in this photo taken on Christmas morning 1988. Bottom row: Kent and Lucas. Top row: Brandon, Garrett and Dixie.

Leta Royer picks up the sheets that were stripped off her bed when the twister tore through her home outside of Haven. Photo by Sandra J. Watts of The Hutchinson News.

'Mom, I'm scared.'

— Lucas Fisher

obliteration of his childhood home.

"I grew up over there, and we sold it to Toby and Wilma Yoder, a young Amish couple, less than three years ago. They had just finished remodeling the big farm house, and it looked so nice," Brauer said. "There were outbuildings, and trees . . ."

Until now, the tornado hadn't totally claimed a house, although some were damaged beyond repair. It was different at the home of Toby and Wilma Yoder.

"I saw it down on the ground and the clouds rolling," the 22-year-old mother of two said. "We took the children and went to the southwest corner of the basement."

"It was coming straight towards us," Toby Yoder said. "I figured it might hit, but I didn't think it would do so much damage."

As they knelt with their heads down and the children under and between them, the Yoders heard the roaring storm tear their house apart. Mud plastered everything around them.

"We knew when the sub-floor went, because it was dark in the basement and suddenly everything was light," Wilma said.

Toby Yoder climbed out first, not expecting the extent of the devastation. "Everything's gone!" he told Wilma in disbelief.

Just half a mile northeast of the Yoders' farm was the beautiful farm home of Lynn and Kathy Geffert. The remodeled two-story home had been built by Lynn's grandfather in 1900-1904. Beside it stood a huge cedar believed to be around a hundred years old. It was one of many trees in the neatly landscaped yard.

Kathy first heard a television weather bulletin about the tornado when it was on the ground near Castleton. About ten minutes later, the sirens went off in Haven, two-and-a-half miles south and a mile east. Kathy hurried out to find her husband, a full-time farmer.

At that moment, Lynn Geffert drove into the yard. Although they couldn't see the unusual cloud to the southwest because of the trees around their yard, they could hear it.

"It was the sound that made me realize it was a tornado. It looked more like a rain cloud, but the sound was like a freight train."

The Geffert's daughter Keri was at home with them, but their son Kyle had stayed in Haven for a football scrimmage. Hoping and praying Kyle was doing the same, the Geffert family ran for cover in the southwest corner of their basement.

Until the moment when a blast of wind blew the windows out, Geffert was convinced the tornado wouldn't hit them. The first blast was followed by a few seconds of relative calm, and then another, stronger blast.

"We heard the house being torn, so I guess we were kind of prepared to see a lot of damage on the house," Kathy said, "but we weren't prepared for the rest."

The farm as they knew it was gone. Nearly all the trees, including the old cedar, were destroyed. Everything that their business as farmers depended upon was either wrecked or would need repairs. Seventeen of

Amish from Yoder, Garnett and Chouteau, Okla., came to help Toby and Wilma Yoder clean up and rebuild their home two miles northeast of Haven. Photo by Carol Duerksen.

their registered Herefords were either dead or had to be killed. One end of the house had blown out. Yet one fact overrode the Gefferts' dismay: All four of them were unharmed.

Already on the ground an unusually long time, the tornado continued on a northeasterly course, slapping trees, farms and homes around with a vengeance. Torturing hundreds of large cottonwood trees along the Arkansas River, it crossed the Reno-Harvey county line.

"I was at the sheriff's office in Newton when the U.S. Weather Service said the tornado was at Castleton," Deputy Sheriff Steve Bayless recalled. "As a road deputy, it was my responsibility to help track the storm if it came into Harvey County.

"I was on the north side of the storm, and another one of our deputies was on the south side. We were calling in reports on the location of the storm each of us was seeing, and the locations were different. But it was the same storm, it was just so big!"

"I've seen a lot of tornadoes in my 17 years in law enforcement, and they are all quite predictable in appearance. They are wide at the top and narrow down to a vortex that touches the ground. This one was different. It didn't have a point — just a big wide base hugging the ground. It's the biggest thing I've ever seen."

In Harvey County, the tornado at times was more than a half-mile wide.

Sharon Baumann watched the storm approaching their home on the Reno-Harvey county line for about 20 minutes, wondering if she should wake her sleeping husband Allen. "I finally decided I'd better wake him. I said 'Honey, get up. There's a tornado and I think it's two miles away,' " she remembered.

The Baumanns had no way to get their 200-pound quadriplegic son Robert into the basement, so they helped him lie down on the floor upstairs and covered him with pillows and blankets. The tornado came through, claiming outbuildings and windows in the house. The three Baumanns emerged unscathed, only to hear shortly afterward that another funnel might be in the area. "That's when Robert said, 'Just throw me down in the basement. I can't feel anything anyway. I'm not going through that again.' " Sharon said. "Thank goodness that second storm never came through."

The Baumanns had, however, suffered more damage than they realized at the time. Another farmstead they owned just down the road lay in a pile of rubble. The house — badly damaged but repairable — stood alone amidst the remains of a barn, sheds, grain bins and fences.

A mile northeast of the Baumann's, 83-year-old John Devenpeck sat scrunched under the stairway in his basement. "I heard the weather man say 'Take cover,' so that's what I did," he said. He heard "a whistling sound" as the storm invaded his home, then found himself trapped in his haven. Finally able to wriggle out of a crawl space about 10 inches wide, Devenpeck walked out of his trashed house to find buildings, fences, trees and machinery lying in disarray in unnatural

'It was coming straight toward us.'

— Toby Yoder

13

Only one wall remains of this house (in photo at right) north of Haven a few hours after the tornado. Photo by Tony Brauer.

The stump of a century-old cedar tree and a gaping hole in the Lynn Geffert home northeast of Haven give silent testimony to the destructive power of a few tornadic seconds. Photo by Ron Perkins.

positions around the yard.

A mile north of John Devenpeck's, Deputy Bayless continued plotting the storm. He watched in horror and awe as the monster storm sucked up Cecil Mitchell's mobile home, garage and outbuildings, and spit them out again in shreds. The next homes in its path belonged to Paul Wedel and Kent Fisher.

Earlier that day, Lucas Fisher, son of Kent and Dixie Fisher, treated his first-grade classmates at Burrton Elementary School to cupcakes for his birthday. March 13 wasn't actually his birthday, June 5 was, but since his was a summer birthday, he and his mother, a registered nurse, decided to celebrate it in school that day. It would be Lucas' last celebration.

After school, Lucas and his older brothers Garrett and Brandon came home to their brick house two miles south and a half mile east of Burrton. Surrounded by trees, the house was barely visible from the road. Across a pond to the east of them lived their great-grandparents, Paul and Cecil Wedel.

Dixie's husband, Kent Fisher, had left for his evening shift at the post office in Wichita, and she joined her sons outdoors. At 5 p.m. they came in to watch "The Wonderful World of Disney." She saw a tornado warning and turned on the radio. When she heard that a tornado was passing through Haven, seven miles away, Dixie sent her sons to the basement.

The phone rang. It was the Wedels: They were coming over. Dixie waited while the elderly couple walked the several hundred yards between the two homes, then hurried them into the southwest corner of the

basement alongside her sons. She felt her ears pop, and heard Lucas, her youngest, say, "Mom, I'm scared."

"Come here," she replied. Then the electricity went off.

"I don't remember the sound of the storm," Dixie said later, her voice trembling. "I heard the sound of cement crunching and bricks falling in from the chimney upstairs. It was pitch black. I began calling names. 'Mr. Wedel. Mrs. Wedel. Garrett. Brandon.' They all answered. 'Lucas.' Lucas didn't answer."

Bricks from the fireplace had fallen on the huddled group. With a flashlight, Dixie saw that Garrett's leg was caught; she could not find Lucas.

"I kept thinking maybe he'd run someplace, and we called and called. Then we started digging. Bricks kept falling on us, and we kept taking them away."

Dixie Fisher finally found her son buried under the bricks. There was no heartbeat. Lucas had died instantly of a broken neck. The tornado had claimed its first human life — that of a bright-eyed, lively, loving six-year-old boy.

Pale in contrast to the young life it had stolen from their arms, the tornado also ravaged the Fisher home and left the Wedel farmstead wrecked beyond repair. At that point, Bayless realized the other deputies were busy checking homes for injured persons, and someone needed to continue plotting the storm.

"At 5 p.m., I called the Communication Center in Newton and told them to sound the storm sirens in Hesston and Moundridge," Bayless said. "I knew the storm was heading in the direction of those towns, and

The Bontragers' "Garden Spot" sign is seen as amended on the day after the tornado. Photo by Janice Camp.

they needed to warn the citizens to take cover."

While Hesston and Moundridge received their first warnings, 76-year-old Eli Bontrager and his wife Opal, 74, watched the storm from their farm two miles north of Burrton. "Opal said 'let's go to the basement' and I thought we should go to the storm cellar," Bontrager said. "But for some reason we got in the car and drove away instead."

Perhaps the decision to drive was providential; when the Bontragers returned, their house was gone, and a farm trailer had been thrown into the basement. Part of the house and the trunk of an elm tree measuring three feet in diameter blocked the storm cellar door. The remainder of the farm looked like a war zone.

Near the Bontragers, the Larry Flickinger farmyard included homes for Larry's family and for his 84-year-old mother Ella. In the familiar pattern, the storm claimed all but the houses, and left them badly damaged.

As Bayless continued to follow the storm and call in its location, a knot grew larger and larger in his stomach. His home northwest of Burrton lay directly in the path of the immense tornado.

"I knew my wife and daughter weren't at home, so I decided not to try to get home," Bayless said. "I stayed behind the storm. Shortly before it hit our place, I called the Communication Center and told them to activate the Hesston and Moundridge sirens again."

Almost as if to say "So there!" the tornado left

Bayless' newly remodeled mobile home behind in a pile of rubble and set its sights on Hesston. Deputy Bayless would have the last word in his battle with the storm over the town, but that was still 10 miles and a dozen farms away.

As if feeding an insatiable appetite, the tornado gorged itself on roofs, barns, fences, trees, sheds and small buildings. Often it left homes badly damaged, and owners emerged from basements to face the unexpected decision and hassle of repairing or building new. The Kenneth Holdeman, Art Koehn, and Bill Toews families had to begin anew rebuilding on the same site — a task all too familiar to Bill and Annie Toews.

"Five years ago, lightning hit our house and it burned down," Bill Toews said. "This time we lost 10 farm buildings, the silo, house, about 200 trees, and 70 sheep. A lot of stuff has happened to us in the eight years we've been married. We have two sons, and no one was hurt in the fire or the tornado. We've realized what really matters in life. We're real easy-goin' people after all this."

The Kenneth H. Stucky farmstead knew all about repeated disasters too. Its first tornado hit occurred in 1942, followed by a twister in 1974 that claimed everything except the house. This time the cloud of fury swallowed up house and garage as it marched on its violent journey.

Deputy Bayless continued plotting the storm as it neared Hesston, calling in its location to the Communication Center. When it moved into Hesston, he

Steve and Vicki Bayless lost their home, many trees and part of a shed at their home northeast of Burrton. One of their knives was found several hundred feet away, stuck in a tree. Photo by Carol Duerksen.

Henry and Eileen Berndsen are grateful they didn't take shelter in their storm cellar: The violent whirlwind pulled the pulley up, opened the cellar door and threw flying debris into the dugout. Eileen was safe inside the house's basement and Henry was enroute home when the tornado hit. Photo by Carol Duerksen.

The tornado gathers strength northeast of Burrton. Photo by Kim Krehbiel.

The Lynn Geffert family stands on what used to be the front door of their house, which was destroyed by the tornado.

noted the tornado would miss Hesston College, a nursing home, retirement center, and trailer court. From his parked car one-half mile behind the storm, he could see the city water tower swaying back and forth.

Five minutes later, as Deputy Bayless followed the tornado out of Hesston to the Harvey-Marion county line several miles away, he had no idea how valuable his warning calls had been. Miraculously, no one in Hesston was killed or even seriously injured as the tornado wreaked its havoc on 150 homes and two dozen businesses. Bayless' warnings had helped prepare the city for the tornado's wrath, and later he felt that in some way, it was he — and not the tornado — that had the last word.

Within minutes of the tornado's terror, the small farming communities of Pretty Prairie, Castleton, Yoder, Haven and Burrton began to rally around their stricken members. As the initial moments of relief and assistance turned into hours and days, the storm's victims were awed by the amount of help they received and dismayed by the incredible stress those few tornadic seconds had brought to their lives.

Five months after the tornado invaded the lives of Floyd and Polly Fry, Floyd sat on the workbench in his new machine shed and reflected on what they had come through, and were still experiencing.

"I didn't know a man could cry so much in three days, but after the tornado, it was just there. For days and weeks afterwards, when I'd come out here to work, I just wanted to turn around and leave. But I

didn't know where to go.

"It wasn't that we weren't getting help. My goodness, it wasn't that at all. There were so many people here — I have no idea how many. Many of them I knew, but many I didn't. That first morning a man I didn't know stopped and said, 'I want to help you, but I can't come help clean up, so I want to give you this.' He handed me a folded bill. I didn't look at it until later. It was $100. I have no way to thank him — I don't know who it was.

"One day a bunch of men decided to build a half mile of pasture fence plus a corral. They cut the hedge posts from the trees, put them in the ground, and strung the wire — all in one day.

"My insurance man told me, 'You'll have to learn that people want to give and they get a blessing from it. You'll have to receive.' And my preacher said, 'Floyd, this is your time to receive.'

"I've given many times when I've gone out on Mennonite Disaster Service trips. But then you leave it there. This time I can't. We always come back to it."

Polly echoed her husband's sentiments, saying the stress has been tempered by gratitude for those who have helped.

"We had so many trees down, and the township spent four days here with their big cats, pushing them together and burning them. I don't know what we would have done without them.

"Some Amish came in and plowed the fields with their rubber tires so we wouldn't have to worry about flats that first time working the fields." (The Amish near

The home and outbuildings of John Devenpeck three miles south of Burrton were damaged beyond repair. After the tornado, Devenpeck (at right in photo) visits with two friends. Photos by Boneva Hammar.

Yoder do not use air tires on their farm equipment. All equipment runs on hard rubber tires to help ensure that the slower vehicles are used for work purposes only.)

John Devenpeck like Polly Fry was uncertain whether to rebuild, but others moved swiftly. Steve and Vicki Bayless moved a new mobile home on to the same site. The Bontragers bulldozed their house and moved to Hesston.

Kathy Geffert agreed with Polly Fry that making decisions about building a new home under the circumstances was difficult.

"It's not fun and exciting to build a new house in this situation," Kathy said. "We didn't have time during the summer to think much about the house because we were so busy trying to get the farm going again. Flat tires? You bet. We're on a first-name basis with Gullickson Tires in town since the tornado.

"We always didn't like depending on people. We were the independent type. But this was something bigger than ourselves, and we were very grateful for all the help we got."

For the Gefferts' neighbors Toby and Wilma Yoder, the cleanup was followed immediately by a "frolic" — Amish terminology for a community gathering to put up a building. Three days after the tornado, Amish arrived to begin digging a basement for a new house. Three months and three days after the storm, the Yoders moved in.

"How the community helped us will always stand out in our minds," Toby Yoder said.

For Kent and Dixie Fisher, the days after the tor-nado were a blur of grief. "Faith in the Lord, friends and family is what helped us get through those days, and what still helps us today," Dixie said. "We've received so many cards of support from other families who have lost a child at one time or another. People from Burrton, the community and nearby churches have all been so wonderfully supportive."

One consistent thread of support and assistance weaving its way through the lives of the victims was Mennonite Disaster Service. Many of the families knew MDS workers were on the scene, cleaning and rebuilding. Some only knew that many, many people were helping. MDS also provided financial support to victims.

"This world's in bad shape," Floyd Fry commented. "But when something like this happens, you realize how many good people there are. I don't know what we would have done without them." □

'Faith in the Lord, friends and family is what helped us through those days.'

— Dixie Fisher

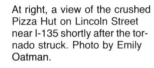

At right, a view of the crushed Pizza Hut on Lincoln Street near I-135 shortly after the tornado struck. Photo by Emily Oatman.

Scenes from Interstate 135

Overturned trucks and a crushed Pizza Hut are shown in the top photo. In the middle photo, help comes streaming into town. Photos by Betty Augustine. At left, this photo by Peggy Weiland shows some of the damage to the Heritage Inn and other property on Lincoln.

At far left, the "Please Wait to be Seated" sign at the Pizza Hut stands upright as volunteers survey what is left of the structure, as seen in this photo by Mark De-Graffenreid. Pizza Hut was one of the first businesses to rebuild. The company built a new restaurant on the same site, seen in the inset photo by Joel Klaassen, and was open for business again on April 19, less than 40 days after the March 13 tornado. A new Phillips 66 truck stop was built next to the Pizza Hut, replacing the destroyed Save-A-Trip.

A group watches in awe as the tornado approaches Hesston as seen in this photo by Duane Graham taken seven minutes before the tornado struck.

Smoke billows from the home of Mel and Mildred Martens at 406 N. Weaver late Tuesday afternoon, about 20 minutes after the tornado hit. Photo by Duane Graham.

The Tornado Explodes Through Hesston

Less than a mile from one another, the two men faced west and watched. One was awestruck by the raging, black mass. The other was sickened by it.

J. Pat Kearney of Wichita, standing beside his company car, waited until the source of his fascination was centered in his Nikon's viewfinder. Then, with careful deliberation, he shot his last frame of film. He didn't hear a sound. The flow of adrenaline had shut out the tornado's roar.

Randy Stauffer of Hesston pounded on the window of his Dodge truck, hearing nothing but his own screams as the twister slammed through his neighborhood.

For a brief moment the men were held captive by the scene they were sharing, watching the debris-filled tornado skate from the east edge of Hesston over the I-135 interchange on its northeast path.

Then the spell was broken. The appearance of flashing lights on emergency vehicles speeding northbound jerked Kearney's attention from the boiling fury to his family in Wichita, where storms also reportedly were threatening. At the same time, Stauffer drove around the two patrol cars that had been stemming the stream of northbound freeway traffic and rushed the few hundred yards to his house — except that now it was nothing more than an open hole in the ground.

Neither man knew he had just witnessed the most tenacious tornado in Kansas history, that it had already killed six-year-old Lucas Fisher of Burrton and soon would take the life of Ruth Voth of rural Goessel.

The city of Hesston was warned of the impending danger with the sounding of the first siren about 5 p.m. Curious residents stepped out to watch, while others began to record on film and video cameras the oncoming funnel cloud. At 5:25 p.m., the second siren sounded. By then, the tornado was nearly upon the city, and people, many reluctantly, had been driven to take cover.

One of the last to take shelter was Tyler Estes, who was sent home from the Hesston High School track field by a coach when the warnings sounded. Estes, who recalled the day's events later in a paper for his junior English class, watched as the tornado entered town.

"It came in from the southwest, and we saw the K-State research center blow apart," he remembered. "I could see the tornado very well, and it looked like there were little birds flying around in it. As it came closer it became apparent that the objects were not little birds, but large pieces of debris."

The time the tornado struck town was estimated to be 5:37 p.m. The clock at Hesston Machine and Welding, owned by Gene and Stan Swartzendruber, stopped when the structure was hit at 5:41 p.m.

Kearney and Stauffer were not aware that in the two-and-a-half minutes that it took the vicious tornado to traverse the picture-postcard-perfect community, 16 people had been injured, 21 businesses and 226 single- and multi-family dwellings were damaged or destroyed — Stauffer's among them.

At that point Stauffer didn't care that he was among

'Then a sound like dynamite filled the air, and our windows blew out.'
— Melissa Davis

Jim Vequist of Hays took this series of dramatic photos north of Hesston near I-135 and Ridge Road over a ten minute span. The tornado is seen in the air, moving northeast, at left. In the center photo, the funnel is captured spewing debris. At right the tornado is seen just after it left Hesston. A traveler standing near the overpass can be seen in lower right of the last photo.

'I got to the driveway and the house was gone.'

— Randy Stauffer

the estimated 300 people who had been instantly rendered homeless. His only thought was to reach his wife, Pat, and his two young daughters.

"It took me awhile to orient myself to where my house was," he said. "I got to the driveway and the house was gone. I went to the edge of the basement stairway and started screaming for Pat."

He found her huddling in the basement with three-month-old Emily and four-year-old Erin. Though only the inside walls of the bathroom and three bedrooms remained, his family was safe.

City Councilman Bob Davis also returned to find his family safe, but his home virtually destroyed. His wife, son Matt, and daughter Melissa had sought refuge in the basement. There was a brief calming, and then "the wind came up suddenly," Melissa wrote three weeks later, also in a paper for her English class. "I noticed that my ears were feeling a lot of pressure and were starting to hurt. Parts of our ceiling were falling, and one part even hit me on the back. I tried to close my ears with my fingers and screamed really loud. Then a sound like dynamite filled the air, and our windows all blew out," she wrote.

The three climbed out over rubble to find only one wall of the house standing. Minutes later Davis arrived home. "He ran to us in our yard and cried really hard, too," Melissa remembered. "He was so happy just to see all of us alive, and for a minute we forgot about the house we had just lost."

Miraculously, everyone in Hesston was alive, and one by one, residents began surfacing like prairie dogs

from whatever means of protection they had sought. Fifteen people emerged from the walk-in cooler of the leveled Pizza Hut restaurant where Jason Reynolds, manager, and John Anderson, assistant area manager for the county franchisee, had convinced them to seek safety.

One of the 15 was Pizza Hut employee Jason Chaffee, another Hesston High School junior. After radio reports of tornado sightings, "I was scaring the waitress with the thought of the tornado being about ready to hit us," Chaffee wrote. "I was joking and having fun as we made pizzas up to the last minute." Any hint of humor fled when the group emerged from the cooler. "At that moment my heart sunk, for I was in shock," Chaffee recalled.

Twelve people who had been led to the hallway of the Heritage Inn by its owner, Claridy Stauffer, walked out of her battered motel without a scratch. While some folks found their neighborhoods untouched, others met with the horror of total destruction.

Destruction could be called Lon Buller's stock in trade. He is a 10-year veteran of emergency preparedness and director of the Harvey County Municipal Division of Emergency Preparedness. His job is to activate the forces needed to take control of a disaster situation and to create order out of chaos. Yet at 5:50 p.m., when Buller arrived in Hesston where he resides with his wife and daughter, he was stunned by what he found. The tornado had missed his house by a mere two blocks.

Left: Workers begin clearing debris at Hesston Decorating Center. Photo by Duane Graham.

The farm house of Richard and Charlene Janzen, located a mile west of town, begins to burn in the final chapter of the demolition process weeks after the tornado. The Janzens now live in Hesston. Photo by Richard Janzen.

"It was one of the toughest sights I've ever run into," he said. "Hesston was literally like a war zone."

Like Lon Buller, Tyler Estes likened Hesston to a war zone. "Cars and semi-trucks were scattered about and destroyed, and the only thing left of houses were concrete slabs and basements. The air was full of police, ambulance and firetruck sirens, and there were gas leaks emitting loud hissing sounds," he wrote.

The tornado had ripped a path between 100 and 200 yards wide across the tidy community, entering at the midpoint of its west side. It left its damaging signature on the Mennonite Brethren Church. As it raged on its northeasterly journey, it blasted residences, the Delta and Pineland seed research facility, Troyer's Furniture and Restoration, Reimer Plumbing and Heating, The Source, Hesston Electric, Hair Designs, Kropf Lumber Co., Hesston Veterinary Clinic, Ole Town Cleaners, Paul's Inc., Pizza Hut, Hesston Heritage Inn, the Sav-A-Trip convenience store and a car and truck wash, among others. It was a vision even someone accustomed to disaster had to struggle to comprehend.

"The first questions I asked myself," continued Buller, "were 'what do we do?' and 'Where do we even begin to start?' "

They were the same questions many people were asking themselves. In the tornado's wake, there was no time for reflection. The grief and sorrow and sense of loss would have to wait until Hesston could begin to absorb the blow that nature had just dealt it.

Sharon Swartzendruber had already begun assessing her situation and it sobered her. She and her four-

year-old son, Brett, had gone to the basement of their white, two-story farmhouse that skirted the edge of town after her husband, Stan, had spotted the tornado from where he had been working on the roof of Sunglo Feed. Stan stopped to phone his wife and warn her to take cover, then he fled south toward Newton in his vehicle.

Sharon couldn't see the tornado coming.

"I had no fears," she said. "To me there wasn't anything to worry about." However, she heeded her husband's advice. Crouching in front of the upright deep freezer, Swartzendruber turned her tow-headed son into her body and shut her eyes to shield them from the cattle manure and barnyard debris that struck them as it flew through the basement door. When they opened their eyes, they discovered blue sky. Nothing of the house that had been built by Stan Swartzendruber's great-great grandfather was left on the foundation. The barn, granary and machine shed had been demolished. The beautiful trees that had graced the 15-acre homestead were either uprooted or stripped and broken.

Almost immediately it seemed as if she could hear her neighbors, Charlene Janzen and her son David, yelling for her. Their farm, directly north across the dirt road, also was heavily damaged.

Swartzendruber could see that a battered line of old oak trees had snared the living room carpet, pieces of the antique furniture she had painstakingly refinished, and some of the family's clothing.

The farm wasn't the only precious thing the

Above: Ernst Wiens in glasses in center of photo, is surrounded by exchange students from Hesston College, on the day after the tornado at the Roupp Apartments. A boy views the devastation from the second floor window. Photo by Vada Snider, Ark Valley News.

Signs tell the story in these two photos. At left, the Roupp family manages to display a dash of upbeat humor in their announcement of revised plans for the family's picnic. Photo by Bob Latta, Hesston Record. Right, another upbeat approach is seen on this sign scrawled on the Roupp Apartments. Photo by Paul Roupp.

The water tower and power lines served as a collecting point for debris. Photo by Duane Graham.

Swartzendrubers were to lose. Hesston Machine and Welding, the business that Stan owned with his father, also was devastated. It had been nested in the center of a concentration of Hesston small businesses that had been in the tornado's path.

Next to the Swartzendrubers' business had stood the spacious warehouse that held Wilma and Jerry Troyer's furniture refinishing business where they both worked. Troyer's Furniture and Restoration, which had been started eight years before in the couple's garage, had grown into a thriving enterprise. About two-thirds of the steel-girded metal building was stuffed with antiques that had been brought to them by customers from as far as McPherson and Wichita.

The Troyers occasionally had discussed what they would do in case of a storm and had agreed that they would go to the small office area in the center of the building, but as the tornado bore down on the warehouse, Jerry and his part-time employee, Bob Glick, ran to a neighbor's house instead. Glick left his saw running. It was found among the ruins with a hole in it. Only an intact chair and a few hand tools remained unscathed. The steel beams had been torn from the concrete in which they had been set. The small office in the center of the warehouse that was to be the Troyers' safe haven was nowhere to be found.

Judy DeWitt had stayed home from work with a headache. As the first warning siren sounded, she went outside with her camera but she, like Swartzendruber, couldn't see the tornado. Even after she took a friend's advice and moved to the basement of her rented house

with her daughter, Jennifer, she watered her plants and listened to the radio without concern. More phone calls alarmed her, and she and Jennifer covered themselves as best they could with a black rubber mat. They heard the splintering of wood and shattering of glass.

"I thought we were going to be sucked out," said DeWitt. "I kept talking to Jennifer, making her tell me she was all right." Then, darkness.

"Once the lights went out, it was over," said Jennifer.

Added her mother, "When we pushed the stuff off of us, there was only the sky. It's such a strange feeling to know your house is completely gone."

The basement stairs were gone as well, so the two crawled out of the mud-drenched hole by climbing onto the washing machine that had been hurled across the room. DeWitt's husband, Ed, wasn't aware that the tornado had hit his home. The radio at Hesston's Excel Industries where he works went off when the tornado cut electrical power. It wasn't until he neared the cul-de-sac where his house and nine others had stood that morning that he realized what had happened.

The Swartzendrubers, Troyers and DeWitts, in addition to the hundreds of other tornado victims in and around Hesston, had forged an unspoken alliance through tragedy. Their stories of loss wove a common thread among them. Yet tragedy would not be able to hold them in its grip for long. They, like every citizen of Hesston, would demonstrate a strength and resiliency that characterizes a community that would continue to survive — with the help of friends.

Left: Residents begin the painstaking search for prized possessions in this northeast Hesston residence. Photo by Mark DeGraffenreid.

"Total Loss" is the caption given this photo by Larry Swank of a building that was left with only its steel structure after being hit with the full force of the tornado's winds, estimated at 250 miles per hour when the tornado plowed through Hesston.

Mildred Martens found out about friends as, still dazed, she realized she had been walking barefoot over the glass strewn throughout her ravaged red-brick home.

"I looked down and said 'I don't have any shoes,' " she recalled. Within minutes a neighbor came running to her with the only pair of shoes that she would wear for the next two weeks.

"Then I said I was cold," she remembered. And almost instantly someone handed her a jacket that she also used for several days.

Some residents, like high school student Greg Sawin, were out of town when the tornado hit, and felt confusion and even guilt upon returning and learning that their homes had been spared. "Only a piece of tin in my yard," Sawin wrote later. "That was our damage, yet others were left homeless.

"One confusing thought I had was a question for God. Why? Later I accepted the fact that the storm was an act of nature, not an act of God. The acts of God came mostly after the tornado during the cleanup. God's face glowed throughout the torn town of Hesston in the following days and weeks. The cleanup was phenomenal. There were people here to help from all over the United States and from all walks of life," he wrote.

It was the selfless gestures during those frightening few moments after the tornado struck that set the tone for the cleanup effort that was already beginning. It was an atmosphere of brotherhood, empathy and, most of all, action.

Shortly after the tornado swept through the city, emergency crews from Newton arrived to conduct the first of three searches to account for every citizen in the county who might have been threatened. Sheriff's deputies canvassed residences outside of the city while other groups went from house to house.

By day's end, Kansas Gov. Mike Hayden had made a driving tour of Hesston and declared Harvey County and seven other counties disaster areas, clearing the way for federal disaster assistance. Fifty members of the 1st Infantry Battalion, 137th Infantry of the Kansas Army National Guard, arrived to safeguard the vulnerable property of the victims. The Hesston Fire Department had been converted into a command center where amateur radio operators brought generators and radio gear to assist with the onslaught of inquiries about the well-being of residents.

The community of Hesston, where the goodness in every situation is attributed to the grace of God rather than to luck, put its deeply held religious convictions into practice. Families, friends and acquaintances opened their doors to their homeless neighbors.

The Midway-Kansas Chapter of the American Red Cross and the Salvation Army established a disaster shelter at Hesston High School, preparing for a massive wave of needy victims. But on that first night, though the Salvation Army did provide food and respite for about 100 people, just seven of the 120 cots the Red Cross had readied for tornado victims were occupied, according to the statistics maintained by Harvey

'One confusing thought I had was a question for God. Why?'
— Greg Sawin

Smashed cars had no chance against the tornado's winds, while the structure of King Construction, in the background, remained standing. Photo by Vada Snider.

The tornado left little work for the salvage yard after it compacted this vehicle into a ball on the west side of Hesston. Photo by Duane Graham.

County's emergency preparedness department. The second night after the disaster, the cots were filled only by guardsmen, and later in the week, by 20 out-of-town young people who had come to Hesston to help with the cleanup.

"We sheltered more workers than victims," observed Mike Wemmer, manager, emergency social services for the Red Cross. "It was a very unusual situation."

Although its resources were stretched throughout seven counties and Red Cross figures reflect records kept on the entire path of cleanup activity, Wemmer estimates that the organization assigned 75 to 80 percent of the volunteers and paid staff to the city of Hesston. Workers met with the victims, assessed their needs and wrote out purchase orders to provide the basic items needed to maintain a household, providing direct assistance to 112 families. During its involvement in the relief effort, the Red Cross collaborated with a network of agencies to serve almost 14,000 meals.

Harvey County had sustained nearly $25 million in damages, close to $22 million in the city of Hesston. Vehicle damage and destruction alone approached $715,000 in the county. The numbers were overwhelming. So was the outpouring of help.

"Hesston had a much higher percentage of destroyed homes than usual," said Wemmer, who has covered nearly 30 major disasters with the Red Cross since 1972. "But Hesston was a model disaster — if you could describe it that way — in that there was a total involvement of community members in assisting

each other. I haven't seen that kind of total commitment in my entire career."

The Mennonite Disaster Service (MDS) seemed to materialize out of nowhere. That came as no surprise to Hesston, the community where the organization had been born 40 years earlier in the Pennsylvania Church, now called the Whitestone Mennonite Church. Volunteers of the civilian program, designed to help victims of natural disasters, arrived by the busload while others, armed with trucks and tools and boundless energy, came on their own. Thousands of MDS volunteers labored along the tornado's path, according to the Mennonite Weekly Review.

"It was a real effort," said Irvin Harms, MDS coordinator of the Hesston area effort. "People came from all over, from places where we'd helped as long as 10 and 15 years ago. We even got calls from Winnipeg, Canada, and Pennsylvania.

On the chilly morning of March 14, all access roads to Hesston, including I-135 exit ramps, were barricaded by guardsmen and Kansas Highway Patrol troopers to keep out curiosity-seekers. Yet for days they would come to stroll through the streets, soak in the devastation and hinder the cleanup effort. Newspaper reporters, television crews and radio reporters singled out families to interview, and their anguish as well as their optimism was splashed on the front pages of local papers and the evening news. Nationally, it seemed as if everyone knew about the event, and strangers sent money, condolences and encouragement.

On that morning, too, the people of Hesston and

UNUSUAL COLORS in this cloud formation over southeast Wichita (shown in the photo at far left) produce an eerie effect shortly before the tornado started near Pretty Prairie, perhaps as a signal of the strange weather yet to come. Photo by Barbara Hilton.

LOOKING SOUTH, one and one-half miles south of Goessel on State Street, this photo shows the funnel as it appears to tower over the Elmer Voth farm. Photo by Herb Schroeder Jr.

CARRYING TONS of debris from its march through Hesston, and with internal wind speeds approaching 200 miles per hour, the tornado is captured in this photo by J. Pat Kearney from the west side of I-135.

THE FUNNEL LOOMS over the Laurel Miller home east of Hesston. At this point, the funnel is still in town and is between one-quarter and one-half mile wide. It passed to the north of the Miller home. Photo by Mike Webb.

PREPARING TO ENTER Hesston, the tornado is seen from Sunset Drive on the northeast side of the city. Photo by Paul Friesen.

THE TORNADO is within two miles of Hesston. The photo at far right by Peggy Wieland, is looking southwest from her home at 748 Lewis Drive.

EMPLOYEES OF KROPF Lumber and Hesston Medical Center watch the tornado's approach to the center of town. The twister destroyed most of Kropf Lumber's buildings. Photo by Emily Oatman.

IN THIS VIEW, from the home of Royce and Sue Enns, one mile east of Hesston, the tornado is shown a few minutes before it entered the city. Photo by Mike Webb.

THE FUNNEL and its supporting cloud formation can be seen in this photo by Ken Kroupa just east of K-17 near Pretty Prairie. At this point the tornado is only a few minutes old.

IN A CLASSIC CONE shape, the tornado rumbles across the Lloyd Funk farm two miles south of Hillsboro on Greenwich Road. Photo by Doug Nelson.

HEADING TOWARD GOESSEL, as seen in this photo taken one mile east of K-15 and one-quarter mile north of the Harvey-Marion county line, the dying Hesston tornado takes on a rope-like shape. Minutes later, it merged with a second tornado, producing a funnel of F5 intensity. Photo by Nancy Franzen.

THE FUNNEL SPEWS out debris it has collected in Hesston as it moves northeast toward Goessel. Photo by Doug Nelson.

BOBBIE HARRIS of Peabody took this two-frame photo two miles east of Hesston which shows the unusual formation of a second tornado.

AN AERIAL VIEW of southwest Hesston shows the beginning of the tornado's devastation where it crossed Knott street, which runs vertically in the middle of this photo. The water tower above is near Knott and old Highway 81, which runs diagonally in the upper left corner of the picture. Photo courtesy of KG&E.

THIS SERIES of photos from Dean Alison's Hesston video, which was shot from just south of the golf course near I-135, shows large parts of houses and buildings exploding with the Hesston water tower in the background.

THE SEVERELY DAMAGED Heritage Inn stands behind the demolished U-Do-It-Car Wash and KFDI radio's mobile unit, which was one of several media units closely involved in the tornado coverage. Photo by Mike Webb.

ONLY A SHELL remains of the Pat Stauffer home at 104 Meadow Lane, which was rebuilt on this location. Photo by Junia Schmidt.

THE SKY ABOVE Hesston High School can be seen from the ravaged southeast bedroom of the home of Alma Pfaust, at the northwest corner of William and Ridge Road, on the day after the tornado. Photo by Tim Travis.

FIRE CAUSED by a broken gas line strikes the home of Mel and Mildred Martens at 406 N. Weaver about 15 minutes after the tornado struck. The house, which was the only one in Hesston to catch fire, was destroyed, and the Martens bought another house in Hesston. Photo by Junior Janzen.

METAL RODS twisted around the remains of this tree on the Jim Moyer farm northwest of Halstead form this unusual, tornado-created sculpture. Photo by Mary M. Beugelsdijk.

THE ROUPP Apartments stand damaged beyond repair in the 100 block of North Roupp Street. Photo by Mike Webb.

A GARAGE ENTRANCE frames a cement truck at what was left of Hesston Concrete, 119 W. Reusser, near the center of town. The business rebuilt on another site. Photo by Mike Webb.

CAROL DAVIS and her daughter, Melissa, survey the remnants of their home at 105 Meadow Lane. None of the Davises were injured. Carol, Melissa and her brother Matt sought refuge in the basement. City Councilman Bob Davis was at work a few blocks away when the tornado struck. The Davises rebuilt on the same spot. Photo by Peggy Wieland.

TORNADO-CHASER and spotter Doug Nelson took this series of photos showing the tornado crossing K-15 a few minutes after it left Hesston. At this point, the twin tornadoes had merged, and the one-half mile wide tornado reached its greatest intensity, F5 on the Fujita scale.
ON THE FARM of Harold and Ruth Voth, (in the large photo above) the Voths' pickup truck lies flattened upside down, surrounded by debris. Photo by Herb Schroeder Jr.

A FLAG and "Yes We're Open" sign are two of the few identifiable items left of the Hesston Decorating Center on North Old Highway 81. A cleanup volunteer helps sort through the debris the day after the tornado. Photo by Larry Swank.

A TREE STUMP stands twisted and frayed after it was snapped in two by the tornado about five miles southwest of Hesston. Photo by Steve Goodyear.

FARM IMPLEMENTS lie in a jumbled, tangled mess on the Voth farm. Photo by Herb Schroeder Jr.

BARREN TREES frame this battered farmhouse three miles south of Goessel on State Street. The house, owned by Don and Ruth Klaassen of Wichita, had been in the Klaassen family for half a century. It was later leveled. Photo by Herb Schroeder Jr.

STUNNED HESSTON residents walk down a war-zone-like street shortly after the tornado. Photo by Betty Augustine. In the photo at top right, **A PIECE OF STRAW** protrudes from this tree on the farm of Eli and Opal Bontrager two miles northwest of Burrton. Photo by Duane A. Graham.

A look through this window on Main Street shows a volunteer clearing debris in a roofless house on Thursday, two days after the tornado. Photo by Vada Snider.

bordering farms were awakening to the incomprehensible task before them.

"Those first few days were a panic," remembered Sharon Swartzendruber. "We asked ourselves things like, 'Where are we going to get our money?' and 'How are we going to eat?' "

Families also needed help in finding and salvaging what precious possessions remained of their lives before March 13. And they were not to be let down. The stark light of dawn found busy volunteers already out in force. More than 700 college students came from Hesston College, Bethel College in Newton, Tabor College in Hillsboro and Bethany College in Lindsborg. Workers came from Newton, Whitewater, Walton, Sedgwick, Burrton, Halstead, Valley Center, Moundridge, the City of South Hutchinson and Hutchinson, and calls offering assistance came from Iola, Emporia, Salina and Dodge City. Inmates from the Kansas State Industrial Reformatory also came to work.

Each day, the labor extended from sunup to sundown and by the weekend, the complexion of the pockmarked community was clearing.

"There was very little left to be done," remembered Buller. "Things were looking more like normal — if you could call it that."

Yet victims were to realize that though there was no shortage of help with the physical labor, their situation was far from normal. They alone had to make the excruciating choices of what to keep and what to surrender to the endless stream of trucks hauling debris to the local landfill.

Said Randy Stauffer, "It was a real struggle to think of all the things we had to do. I don't know if I would make the same decisions that I did then, but at the time you just go through the motions. There was too much to think about. I had 35 people on my property and I didn't know what to tell them."

Hesston Mayor John Waltner said, "We were asking people to make decisions about some very important things. What we wanted to accomplish was to change the visual impact of what had happened as quickly as we could.

"A lot of people made those tough decisions and it happened very fast. But the significance of their losses and the change was something that they couldn't process emotionally then, and may take a long time to come to terms with."

If the victims were able to avoid coming to terms with their emotional reactions to the blow they had been dealt, they were not allowed the luxury of putting off the demands of securing the necessities they needed to get from one day to the next.

Often, their only alternative was to make use of the resources provided by relief organizations. This community, so skilled in the art of giving, was learning a lesson in receiving — and it was not something its proud, self-reliant residents felt easy about.

"We all knew how to give, it's just something you do," remarked Mel Martens. "But it was hard to let people give to us. It was difficult to be a receiver."

Martens and his wife Mildred, however, were to learn about receiving in the most poignant of ways.

'*I don't think we'll ever be back to normal.*'

— Jeannine Hoheisel

Chopped in two, probably by one of the multiple suction vortices in the Hesston tornado, half of this house stands as a strange reminder of the tornado's force. Photo by Bob Latta.

A tree house effect is the treatment the tornado gave to these household goods merged with the remains of a tree. Photo by Vada Snider.

Five years ago, Mildred had befriended a young Hesston woman with two children who was struggling to make ends meet. The Martens had taken the family under its wing and over the years helped out in whatever ways they could.

Mildred remembered the woman asking how she could ever repay her, and Mildred's reply had been to advise her to help someone else if she ever had the occasion. After learning that the tornado had ravaged Hesston, the young woman, her children and her sister traveled from Emporia where they had moved and specifically asked to help the Martens. They spent the day cleaning the yard of the house the Martens had moved into after their home burned when the tornado ruptured its gas line. Then she offered $40 of her income tax return money to the Martens.

"She was still needy," said Mildred. "I knew she probably couldn't afford it. As it turns out, she taught us something, too."

A Kansas City family sent the Martens $10, even though the letter that accompanied the cash revealed it was struggling through hard financial times of its own.

"I don't know that I'll ever spend this ten dollars," said Mel, clutching the letter and wiping tears from his eyes. "Maybe we'll have a chance to send it to someone else who is in trouble someday."

In addition to the money sent by individuals, Dillons Stores, Harvest Food, Cherry Orchard Furniture, Pizza Hut, Gerber Foods and countless other businesses in the state contributed food, bottled water, medical supplies, household furnishings and clothing.

In the first two days, the Salvation Army sent two 26-foot trucks crammed with clothing, bedding and food. Two more trucks arrived in the next two days. In the three days following the disaster, it served 3,000 cups of coffee, 840 doughnuts, 2,500 sandwiches, 500 cold drinks and 820 lunches. From March 14 to March 16, the Army served more than 3,000 meals, according to the figures compiled by Maj. Harry Brocksieck, Wichita city commander.

As money continued to flow into the city from around the country, church leaders from Hesston United Methodist Church, Inter-Mennonite Church, Hesston Mennonite, Mennonite Brethren and Whitestone Mennonite assembled to form the Ministerial Alliance to disburse about $140,000 of donations to everyone who needed financial aid.

The Newton Ministerial Alliance Fund for Tornado Relief, the Hesston Tornado Victims Fund and the Hesston Chamber of Commerce Relief Fund were established to help victims get back on their feet. The Newton Area Chamber of Commerce, the Sedgwick County EMS and First Federal of Newton, among others, accepted cash and donations. And five months after the disaster, the Red Cross had spent nearly $108,000 in victim assistance, almost exactly what it had received from donors, said Mike Wemmer.

As the week following the tornado progressed, and the cleanup quickly gained momentum, townspeople were able to turn their attention to the psychological and emotional trauma that the tornado had inflicted.

Workers salvaging remains on the second floor of the Roupp Apartments are captured in dollhouse style in this photo by Vada Snider.

At the Gene Yoder residence, the salvage operation is under way on the day after the tornado. Photo by Duane Graham.

Schools and churches took up the task of healing through prayer and sharing. A crisis-intervention team was made available to Hesston school children and teachers to help them work through their grief and insecurity.

Ed Zuercher, the high school English teacher who taught Tyler Estes, Melissa Davis and Jason Chaffee, said that in the days following the tornado, the students immersed themselves in writing papers on their experiences.

The purpose of the writing, he said, was two-fold. "When you have a traumatic experience, there is some therapy involved in expressing your emotions through writing. But it's also important for history. By recording very emotional events, you can go back 10 or 20 years later and gain a better perspective than if you just rely on your memory, which is imperfect."

In the last half of 1990, the bound version of the writings by Zuercher's students was one of the most popular volumes at the Hesston public library.

"The tornado really affected the way you talked to people," explained Randy Stauffer. "All your social graces were gone. You said what you thought without thinking about whether it was the polite thing to say or not."

Stauffer's in-laws, Junia and Doris Schmidt, also had lost their home of 15 years to the tornado and the routine of Sunday dinners and family gatherings came to a halt.

"We were used to seeing them every day," he said of his wife's parents, who had been forced to move into a small basement apartment in Newton. "We weren't there to support each other because we were all preoccupied with making the same kinds of decisions."

Instead, Stauffer and his family took comfort in the company of other victims who also took their meals at the central shelter.

"For the first couple of weeks, the best thing we did was to go to the dinners," he said. "It felt good to be with other people. You didn't feel alone. And there was the standard phrase, 'How are you doing?'"

Yet, even with counseling and plenty of sympathetic shoulders ready to share their burdens of loss, victims were to find their road back to normalcy a bumpy one.

Some families were forced to relocate as many as three times before they were able to settle in one place. Many had to face the daunting question of whether to rebuild or move into an existing house, possibly in another town. Though Stauffer's family never had any intention of building a new home, they couldn't deny the deeply embedded roots at 104 Meadow Lane. Rather than live anywhere else, he and Pat chose to rebuild.

Dennis and Jeannine Hoheisel, whose house was severely damaged, were piecing it back together as best they could.

"You have good days and bad days," Jeannine said. "Sometimes you start to look for something and remember where it was and then you remember the way it was, and it's not there anymore. And you think to your-

'You have good days and bad days.'
— Jeannine Hoheisel

The remains of Kropf Lumber after the churning action of the tornado are seen in this photo by Betty Augustine.

A grain elevator on South Main was deflated by the tornado. Photo by Mike Webb.

self, 'Someday there'll be an end to this madness.'

"Actually, I don't know that we'll ever be back to normal," she continued. "It's like you moved a thousand miles and you didn't move an inch."

The DeWitts had been looking for a lot in Hesston on which to build a home before the tornado destroyed their rental house. It shifted their search into high gear. They purchased a lot where the home of Roger and Claridy Stauffer, owners of the Heritage Inn, once stood.

"We bought a basement," said Ed DeWitt dryly, adding that his family intended to store a few blankets, a flashlight and a battery-powered radio — just in case.

Jerry and Wilma Troyer's furniture refinishing business was up and running — back at home in their small garage.

"We got back in operation a lot faster than some of the others," said Wilma of the town's business people. "We have a lot of the victims' furniture to repair and refinish."

Stan and Sharon Swartzendruber were taking their time. Their first priority in the two months following the storm had to be to restore the welding shop to working order and start generating an income again. The family was living in a mobile home near the site where they planned to rebuild. Stan intended to do much of the work himself. Months later, they still were picking up glass and debris from the homestead.

"I think it'll take about two years before things are back to normal and we can have people out for Sunday dinner," Stan said. "And it'll be several years

before the field is clean again."

The Swartzendrubers were grateful for the return of a torn and battered photograph of their son when he was eight months old, which was discovered nearly 60 miles from Hesston in Hope by Lindy C. Riedy of Smith Center.

Riedy wrote, "I know that everyone is thankful their lives were saved, and material things don't mean that much compared to human life. Still, it's the little things, such as pictures, that are missed."

Mildred Martens also was grateful for a small keepsake that her husband managed to recover from the home where they had spent 28 years. He rummaged through the smoky rubble until he found the gold sweetheart bracelet that he had given her when they were courting.

"It really isn't worth much money," she said, as she ran her fingers over the heart in the bracelet's center. "But to me, it's priceless."

J. Pat Kearney, who had coolly stood outside of his car and photographed the tornado as it blistered through Hesston, was intrigued by the history he had captured on film. For days he stewed about what to do with the extraordinary pictures he had taken and, finally, he decided to print his best shot on some T-shirts along with the slogan, "Toto, we're back in Kansas." Reactions to his shirts from others ran the gamut from disapproval to delight.

Once Kearney was able to convince merchants to put his shirts on their shelves, sales were brisk. People often purchased them as gifts for out-of-state friends

Battered, but still proudly standing, is the Stan Carlile residence, a 100-year-old house that was once the home of A. L. Hess, one of the founders of Hesston. Photo by Duane Graham.

Residents begin the cleanup and salvage work at this two-story Hesston home with a gaping hole in the second level. Photo by Mike Webb.

and relatives. One merchant told Kearney that a St. Louis woman bought a T-shirt for a friend of hers who had been one of the munchkins in the movie, *The Wizard of Oz.*

Kearney donated part of his profits to the relief effort and invested some of his proceeds toward his boys' college educations.

"I didn't want the shirts to be gloomy reminders of what had happened," he said. "I've met a lot of different people and heard so many different tornado stories. It's been a very positive, very educational experience."

Though most people would never consider their tangle with the tornado a positive one, the ordeal wasn't without a few lighter moments.

Milt Miller found a pair of his trousers hanging from a tree, still encased in a cleaner bag and undamaged. Kirk Alliman emerged from the ruins of his home to the sound of a ringing phone. It was his mother calling to find out if he was in danger. A Hesston street sign was discovered in Riley County, more than 60 miles away, and returned to the city within a few days.

Randy Bachman, who boards the Brittany spaniel he co-owns with Randy Stauffer, got the dog back after it was whisked away by the tornado. The dog had been sighted around Hesston for several days before it was returned to his owners.

"We didn't give him much of a chance after seeing what was left of his dog pen," said Bachman. "I don't know how he made it but somehow he did."

The tornado's proportions were certain to foster mythical stories as well, such as cows and entire homes being hurled through the sky. And it is no wonder that myths will continue to arise. The unsubduable storm attested to the power of nature and its ability to alter one's perception of the impossible. It shook the town to its foundation about its beliefs in permanence, predictability and continuity.

Old routines were broken and it would take some time for them to be replaced.

"The newness of every little thing is difficult to handle," said Mel Martens, who caught himself more than once driving absent-mindedly to his former address. "You get into a pattern of life, and habits are so ingrained in you, you find it hard to change."

No one in the community of 3,000 views things quite the same now. The capricious sky commands a watchful eye. Homes are no longer bastions of safety. The wind is a fickle friend.

And folks look at their city and each other with a renewed sense of esteem.

Said Jay Wieland, Hesston city administrator, "The face of Hesston has changed forever. Things have occurred in the business community, and we'll continue to see some changes. There is new growth, very positive growth.

"The tornado has made the community as a whole appreciate Hesston as an attractive place, a good place to live. And I think we'll work harder to preserve those things that make it that way."

On October 13, exactly seven months after the

'It will take a lot of living to make this place home.'

— Mildred Martens

Basement cleanup is seen in a different light. Photo by Vada Snider.

Tense emotions are shared as Lena Good is embraced by Bill Hugie a few hours after the Hesston tornado paid its devastating visit. Photo by Vada Snider.

town was ripped apart, Hesston's business community commemorated a new beginning. Enterprises that had been destroyed or damaged opened their doors to the public in celebration.

Hesston now is looking toward the future. Only subtle traces of March 13 remain. New homes gleam from tidy streets. Freshly planted yards are smooth and well-groomed. Young trees have been planted. Residents are busy restoring order in their lives. Indeed, it is the living of each day that seems to heal the wounds of upheaval.

Said Mildred Martens, "It took a lot of living to make our old house a home. And it will take a lot of living to make this place home. But with the help of our family and the grace of God, we made it — and we're going to make it." □

'With the help of our family and the grace of God we made it!'

— Mildred Martens

TORNADO!

TRAVELS SOUTHWEST TO NORTHEAST — USUALLY

OVER OUR HOUSE

REBUILDING TAKES A LONG TIME

NOTHING LEFT AFTERWARDS

ANYTHING CAN BE DESTROYED

DESTRUCTION IS INCREDIBLE

OVERWHELMING

by Matt Bell & Scott Barge

Matt Bell and Scott Borge, students in Mrs. Shannon Zuercher's 7th grade class in Hesston, tell the story of the tornado as seen from their perspective in the verse above.

Unbelievable destruction haunts what once was the home of Harold and Ruth Voth near Goessel. Ruth lost her life in the March 13 tornado. Photo by Brian Stucky.

The March 13 Tornadoes:
The Twister Intensifies As It Nears Goessel

Jon Buller's biggest concern when he left his job at Holstine Chevrolet in Newton at 5:30 p.m. on March 13 was delivering a van before the hail hit. As an ugly cloud massed to the west, he headed north on K-15, the state highway that bisects Kansas from Oklahoma to Nebraska.

Buller's journey was short — only six miles to make his delivery to a farm south of Goessel, a Mennonite farming community of about 500 in south-central Kansas. With the van delivered, Buller jumped into his 1975 Chevy pickup, which he'd left that morning, and headed back to K-15 for the 10-mile drive to his home northeast of Goessel. As he drove north on K-15, Buller watched the churning cloud, the snakes dipping out of it, and the emergence of one massive tornado.

Two miles west of Buller's speeding truck and about five miles northeast of Hesston, Isaac and Esther Ratzlaff watched the storm from their farmstead. Forty-three years of hard work had gone into building the farm that had started with an alfalfa field. Mature elm trees, white fences, the two-story farm home and well-maintained barns and sheds all gave quiet testimony to the Ratzlaffs' appreciation of the land.

Like Buller, the Ratzlaffs saw the two tails merge into one wide bank and then it was close — very close. The Ratzlaffs' made it to the basement, felt an incredibly strong wind, and heard glass breaking. It was 5:40 p.m., and the storm had claimed another farm.

Bent on destruction, the wall of fury bore down on the nearby Carl and Betty Klassen farm, left it looking like a bomb-scape, and moved on. A mile ahead at Iris Lane Dairy, four silos stood out before the approaching cloud. Brothers Fred and Jim Schmidt and their hired hand Roger Campbell watched the storm as they milked their 90-cow herd.

"The guys were standing outside watching it," Diana Schmidt said, "and I started handing stuff to the children in the basement — baby books, purse, wallet, coats and shoes. They had their three favorite cats down there, too. Pretty soon I felt like I needed to be down there with them, but the guys stayed outside. I kept yelling at Jim to come in, and finally they did. On his way down, Jim threw our big collie dog down the stairs to join us — for some reason the dog didn't want to go down. Fred waited until he saw the unoccupied place a quarter of a mile away explode, and then he came tearing down the steps, too."

While Fred Schmidt took shelter at the dairy, his wife Jo-Ann, 13-year-old son Mike, and daughter Rachel watched the storm from their home an eighth of a mile north. Mike had two things to worry about — he was videotaping the tornado and he was trying to convince his mom to open the windows. Jo-Ann, even though she had heard research reports that it didn't make any difference, wanted them closed. When Jo-Ann decided it was time to take cover in their storm cellar, the windows were open.

ElRoy Wiens left work at Cessna in Wichita at 5 p.m. for the 40-minute drive to his farm southwest of Goessel. He heard on the radio that the tornado was approaching Burrton and realized the storm's route

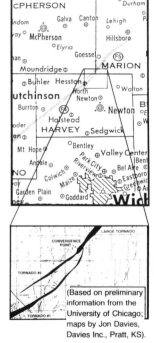

(Based on preliminary information from the University of Chicago; maps by Jon Davies, Davies Inc., Pratt, KS).

BIRTH OF AN F5 TORNADO: While tornado #1 (F4 intensity) plows through Hesston, tornado #2 (F1 or F2 intensity) touches down just northeast of town.

Both tornadoes travel roughly parallel to each other for two miles, then converge. The result is a large tornado which shortly reaches F5 intensity.

In a race against the wind, Jon Buller arrived home just in time to get his wife Shelley and sons Dylan and Travis into the basement. Their house suffered major damage, but after living elsewhere for three and a half months, the Buller family is back on their homestead northeast of Goessel. Photo by Carol Duerksen.

Packing an F-5 intensity (the highest ever recorded by meteorologists), the March 13 tornado crosses Highway 15 a half mile south of Goessel. Photo by Carl Reimer.

'My neighbor said he saw a barn raise up about three barns high and then set back down.'

— Dennis Flaming

would take it close to his home across the road from Iris Lane Dairy. He "ever so slightly" broke the speed limit that day, he said, and when he got within one-and-a-half miles of his home, the tornado loomed between him and his family. As the storm moved on, he drove toward home, but debris stopped him. He got out and began running and, within several hundred yards of his home, passed a neighbor who simply said, "Oh, ElRoy, I'm so sorry."

Torturing hedge rows and flinging debris onto fields, the tornado continued its 100-mile northeasterly march across the flat Kansas farmland. LeRoy and Alice Funk watched it approach their farm and knew they were going to be hit.

By this time, Jon Buller was nearing Goessel. His mind kept telling him to pull over and seek cover, yet his foot never left the floorboard. "I saw the tornado cross Highway 15 a mile behind me. I usually turn east on the paved road that goes past Harold and Ruth Voth's home, and then go north to our place. But this time I kept going north on Highway 15. I knew I shouldn't try to outrun the thing, but I kept on going."

Two miles northeast of Ruth and Harold Voth's, Dennis Flaming and his son John had been watching the tornado for about 20 minutes. Mesmerized by the little tails dancing in and out and the formation of the huge rotating whirlwind, they didn't even think to take pictures. As the storm drew nearer, Dennis noticed a car speeding past his farmstead.

"Who would be out driving now?" he thought. He learned later that his neighbors, Randy and Meribeth

Schmidt, had opted to leave when it appeared their farm was in the funnel's path.

Strangely, several months earlier, Meribeth had awakened from an afternoon nap to a disturbing sight. A blackish twisting vortex seemed to be hovering in the corner of the bedroom near the ceiling. Although she felt no imminent danger, Meribeth, a deeply spiritual church deacon, was upset at the apparition and felt uneasy in its presence.

These strange circumstances repeated themselves approximately four times over the next several weeks. Each time, Meribeth rebuked the invader in the name of God.

Now, as she and her husband fled the storm nearing their home, she wasn't remembering the miniature whirlwinds. She was praying that they and their farm would be spared from one of the largest tornadoes in the history of Kansas.

While Meribeth and Randy left their home behind, Jon Buller continued to speed toward his, anxiously eyeing the tornado in his rear-view mirror. He was just a few miles from home now, and he could feel powerful wind gusts pushing his pickup all over the dirt road. Though he still thought he should pull over and seek shelter in a culvert, he did not. He just kept on going.

Buller's young son Dylan met his daddy on the porch as usual. Buller grabbed Dylan, rushed into the house, and yelled, "Go to the basement!" to his wife, Shelley. Unaware of the approaching twister, she was feeding their other son in the kitchen. Buller ran upstairs for some photo albums and joined his family

Shocking scenes at the Carl Klassen farmstead south of Goessel show what a few moments in the path of a powerful tornado can do. Photos by Brian Stucky.

under a bed in the basement. Less than two minutes after his arrival home, the tornado was upon them.

"Our ears popped, we heard things breaking, and it was over just like that," Shelley remembers. "We came up to find our house was still standing, but the windows were broken and there was glass everywhere, especially in the kitchen, where I'd been with Travis a few minutes earlier. I hate to think of what would have happened if Jon hadn't made it home in time to warn us. It couldn't have been much closer."

Although standing, the Buller's house northeast of Goessel had been slapped around badly. One wall was separated from the structure, and other structural damage would require major repair work. A dog kennel, trees, garage, fences — the yard was a shambles. The cast iron love seat from the front porch was found a half mile away several days later.

Randy and Meribeth Schmidt returned home shortly after the tornado passed. Their farmstead had been spared, but a half mile away an unoccupied farm they owned had been destroyed. Their friends and neighbors, Dennis and Glendene Flaming, weren't as fortunate.

"My neighbor says he saw our barn raise up about three barns high and then set back down," Flaming recalls. "We lost the barn, fences, feeders and the garage. Part of the roof and a wall on the house were damaged pretty bad."

The most tragic scene in the Goessel community was the farmstead of Harold and Ruth Voth. Ruth had visited her husband at Newton Medical Center that

afternoon. They talked about life and death. Harold was recovering from cancer surgery. Recently, he had tried to prepare her for being a widow, just in case. They had talked about funerals and shared some of their wants and preferences in funeral plans.

Ruth went home late that afternoon to their farmstead one-and-a-half miles east of Goessel. No one knows if she saw the powerful, monstrous cloud boiling its way towards her home before she was killed by its fury.

Ruth's body was found along the road, surrounded by the twisted remains of all that she and Harold owned. Absolutely nothing — not even a pile of debris — was left of the home they'd shared for 30 years. Harold and Ruth met in the late 1940s working for the Mennonite Central Committee in Mexico. After returning to Kansas where they were married, the Voths spent much of the 1950s as missionaries in Mexico. In 1960, they moved to the Goessel area, converted an old army barracks into a home and raised three children.

As Harold's brother and pastor walked into his hospital room to break the news of Ruth's death, family members and friends combed the wreckage for anything they could save.

LeRoy and Alice Funk's house survived the onslaught, but the tornado claimed 80 large evergreen trees surrounding their home — trees planted by LeRoy 40 years ago. Destroyed too was a barn and chicken house.

A mile away, ElRoy Wiens ran toward his home,

Stoned describes the condition of Dennis and Glendene Flaming's car following the tornado's violent visit to their home northeast of Goessel. Photo by Brian Stucky.

Tree-lovers LeRoy and Alice Funk lost 80 cedars in the tornado — cedars that LeRoy planted 40 years ago. Flanking them is the stump of a tornado victim, and a new young cedar — one of 80 they have replanted since March 13. Photo by Carol Duerksen.

Hail covered the lawn in front of Goessel High School the evening of March 13; this piece was collected by Brian Stucky. Stucky said pieces this size — approximately 2½ inches in diameter — could be seen "every ten feet or so, and the rest was smaller." The hail fell moments before the tornado marched two miles east of Goessel. Photo by Brian Stucky.

Building an addition to their home was a tornado-forced opportunity for the ElRoy Wiens family south of Goessel. Pictured are Loretta Wiens and son Corey. Photo by Carol Duerksen.

the words "Oh, ElRoy, I'm so sorry," ringing in his ears. The garage was gone and the house damaged, but it was still there. His wife Loretta, daughter Amy and son Corey emerged from the basement, unscathed. The garage, cars, house and other damage could be repaired, he thought. Thank God his family was okay!

Across the road at Iris Lane Dairy, the Schmidt families came out of their basements in a mixture of gratitude and disbelief. They were all safe, but Jim and Diana's big farm house was battered, beaten and full of debris. Fred and Jo-Ann's house stood undamaged, windows still open, but the big barn 50 yards away was destroyed. The dairy's barn and calf hutches were gone, yet all but one of the cattle were alive. A large machine shed lay crumpled upon itself, and straw covered much of the yard. Three of the four silos remained, along with two other buildings in perfect alignment between them and the house.

"I don't know, but I have to wonder if the silos somehow broke the force of the wind and that's what spared the house," Jim speculated. "You just don't know how these things work."

Like other families affected by the storm, the Schmidts walked through the next few days in a daze of decision-making, cleanup, grief and gratitude.

After wrestling with the decision, the brothers chose not to rebuild the dairy. The milk cows were sold, and the families concentrated on the cleanup and repair, which had begun the morning after the tornado when hundreds of volunteers had shown up to help.

"It's the good in us all, isn't it?" Jim said of the outpouring of volunteers.

Jim and Diana Schmidt were part of the Mennonite Disaster Service organization that mobilizes assistance to communities following a disaster. As their local church's contact couple, they had helped send volunteers to stricken areas, and they had gone themselves many times. In fact, many of the tornado victims had gone out on MDS calls in the past and now found themselves on the receiving end.

"I'd been on a lot of MDS trips in 29 years and seen a lot of disasters," Isaac Ratzlaff said. "But this time it was ours. We really couldn't comprehend the help we were receiving."

ElRoy Wiens echoed the same feelings. "As a child, I went on MDS trips with my dad, and I've gone since then too. Until a disaster hits you, you can't realize what you're doing when you help people. We really felt God working through the hands of the people who helped us."

Jon and Shelley Buller, who like most of the victims had spent all their lives in the Goessel area, were also grateful for the concern of family and friends that first night and the next day. But on Thursday, two days after the tornado, Jon Buller found himself cleaning up alone.

"Because our house damage was on the back side, it didn't look bad from the road," Buller said. "Most people didn't realize how extensive it was, or that we'd end up moving out for three-and-a-half months. Going through this will certainly make us more sensitive to

Whipped by the tornado, this uninhabited house south of Goessel was torn down by owners Don and Ruth Klaassen. Photo by Herb Schroeder, Jr.

Trashed describes many farmsteads such as this one near Goessel that bore the invasion of Kansas' violent weather in 1990. Photo by Herb Schroeder, Jr.

other people during a disaster, because we know the kind of stress it puts on a family."

Isaac and Esther Ratzlaff were also forced to move out of their home, and they opted to buy a house in Goessel and retire there.

"We had talked about moving off the farm sometime, and decided when there was a reason to move, we would," Esther said.

His eyes brimming with tears, Harold Voth testified that faith, family and a community of friends had helped him through the loss of his wife and home and his struggle with cancer.

"Some people have said to me that I am in the same position as Job in the Bible," he said, "but I tell them my friends have done considerably better by me than his did. Job's friends gave him useless advice. My friends have prayed for me, supplied my needs and helped me. These people have made God's love understandable, comprehensible and tangible. They bring God to me."

Harold said that in June, after looking for a house in Goessel, he realized that home was the farmstead he had lived on for so long. He put up a metal storage building similar to the one that was destroyed and planned to be in a new home by Thanksgiving. "This is my home, and this is where I want to be for my children and grandchildren." He died in September, however, before his plans were fulfilled.

Leaving devastation in its wake from Pretty Prairie to Goessel, the twister continued to move to the north-east. Ten miles ahead lay Hillsboro, a farming community of about 3,000 in Marion County. Around 6 p.m. just southeast of Hillsboro, Jim and Joyce Thiessen were sitting down for supper on their dairy farm.

I'd heard on the radio that it had hit Hesston," Joyce Thiessen said, "but we had so many trees in our shelter belt we couldn't see anything from the house."

One mile northeast of them, Linden and Dorene Thiessen, Jim's brother and sister-in-law, could see the tornado from an upstairs window of their A-frame house. Linden phoned his brother to warn him that the storm seemed to be headed for the dairy farm.

"About that time it got real quiet outside," Joyce said, "and we could see the dust coming up in the field south of our house. We went to the basement and barely sat down when we could feel the vacuum, and heard the swish of a very hard wind, and heard glass breaking. Then it was quiet. We figured, 'That didn't sound so bad' and went up to look."

But it was bad. Windows were broken and debris littered their remodeled, two-story farm home. The calf barn and calf hutches, a silo, three grain bins, roofs from three freestall barns, trees, and half of the machine shed lay in disarray on the yard. The house roof was torn off where part of the machine shed had rammed into it. The 35-year-old shelter belt no longer blocked the horizon.

Two other people had been on the yard when the storm hit. Hired hand Tim Nuss was in the milk barn, and the milk truck driver had been near the destroyed silo.

'We really couldn't comprehend the help we were receiving.'

— Isaac Ratzlaff

Survivors Linden and Dorene Thiessen cowered from the tornado in their basement, and when they lifted the mattress covering them, they could see the sky where their home had been moments earlier. Another survivor was their "white" cat, being comforted by Don Isaac. Photos by Connie Isaac.

Four silos faced the tornadic fury at Iris Lane Dairy south of Goessel, and three remain standing after the onslaught. Most of the top-producing dairy's other buildings were destroyed, and brothers Jim and Fred Schmidt decided not to continue in the dairy business. Photo by Brian Stucky.

"We were so relieved to find them and see that they were okay," Joyce said. "Tim hit the floor of the milking pit (a lowered alley-way running the length of the barn) when he knew it was going to hit, and the wind pushed him through the pit, but he wasn't hurt. The driver was just getting into his truck when the silo came crashing down beside the truck, but amazingly he was okay too."

While Joyce and Jim surveyed their damage and thanked God no one was hurt, the relentless cloud moved on.

"We'd been watching it for quite awhile," Dorene Thiessen said. "We called Jim and Joyce, and I called my dad in Marion. I jokingly said to him, 'I'll call you back if we're still here after it's over.' "

When Linden and Dorene saw his brother's place go, Dorene hurriedly collected her wedding rings and some other jewelry. Linden put on his best boots, grabbed his new pair of tennis shoes, and together they sought out the basement bedroom that didn't have any windows.

"We got in between the bedsprings and mattress, and held the mattress over our heads," Dorene said. "We were just praying and holding each other tight. We never heard the roar — just the loud creaking of nails being pulled out of wood. At one point, our feet felt light, as if they were being sucked up. When it was over, we lifted the mattress and could see daylight above us."

The house, including the subflooring, was gone. Glass and pieces of two-by-fours rested on the mat-

tress. The door beside them had been sucked off its hinges and out of the basement. Yet they were unharmed.

Wary of downed electrical wires everywhere, Linden crept gingerly out of the basement. After a moment he called back to his wife, "Don't worry about the electrical wires. We don't even have a pole."

Their two-year-old dwelling was demolished — a house Linden (a construction worker) and Dorene built themselves after losing a mobile home and everything in it from a fire on December 26, 1987. Nearly everything on their yard — farm equipment, buildings, fences, round bales — was either damaged or destroyed. Five out of 40 sheep were killed; the four horses apparently had "flown" across the yard and were injured and bleeding. Despite the damage, Linden and Dorene Thiessen were able to laugh at vagaries of the storm.

"We found a big wet spot out by the shed, and we couldn't figure out what it was from, since it didn't rain here," Dorene said. "Then we found a few boards and what was left of the water bed mattress, and the mystery was solved."

Smiling in spite of the loss of home and possessions twice in two years, Linden and Dorene attributed their attitude to two factors.

"We're absolutely convinced God is in control," Dorene said. "And secondly, we've both had experiences in the past that taught us there's something worse than losing your things. People are what really matters. And that's not just a cliche with us — it's a reality of our hearts."

Only moments after the storm passed, the Thiessen

Harold Voth holds part of a quilted wall-hanging that was one of the few keepsakes found after the March 13 tornado destroyed the Voth home and killed his wife, Ruth. The quilt, which had been made by Ruth, was found about 10 miles away. It was cleaned, framed and returned to him in a special presentation only a few weeks before his death on September 15. Photo by Stan Friesen.

families began to receive assistance from individuals, churches, organizations and groups. The Hillsboro Fire Department, Associated Milk Producers and neighboring dairy farmers made it possible for Jim and Joyce to keep their milk cows on the farm and continue milking them. Mennonite Disaster Service volunteers assisted with finances and workers, including seven Canadians, spent two days rebuilding a shed on the dairy farm.

Both families moved to Hillsboro while their new homes were being constructed. The decisions that had to be made quickly regarding the farming operation, as well as the decisions involved in building a new home, were not easy, and the stress increased after the moral and physical support of volunteer workers was gone. "You have to keep yourself going and keep yourself 'up.' I have come to realize the only way to get through this is to depend on the Lord," Joyce said. □

A Voth Relative Remembers

It was all over the radio — "Tornado ripping through south central Kansas." The reports made it sound like an advancing army. You could pinpoint its movement in your mind as it tore across county lines and bore down on small towns and farms.

I never saw the tornado. I followed the gray mass of clouds from Wichita northward. After a call to Hillsboro warning my wife and kids not to go to Newton for piano lessons I headed northwest on old 81 for Hesston. My Uncle Paul and his wife Freda lived there. Their home had been grazed by shrapnel from the twister, boards through their picture window, 2x4s piercing their roof, and their garage door at a crazy angle. But they were safe. I took off for Goessel. My wife Diane had suggested I stop by to check up on my aunt Ruth Voth.

The sky was getting darker but evidence of the storm was still visible, strewn haphazardly across fields and wrapped around trees. A power line was down on K-15 so cars were being routed around the section and through Goessel.

I always looked for that landmark, the red pole barn at the Voths, before I started braking to turn into their drive. Tonight it wasn't there. Nothing was. The only red came from the intermittent flash of emergency lights. There were several cars parked close to the road. I had to get through. "I'm related" got me past the line of cars to where I could park. I ran back to the cluster of people. They parted. I knelt down and touched her face. She looked asleep lying there half in, half out of the ditch by the side of the road. "Why?" I held her for a moment, they don't want you to do that for too long. What was the rush?

I walked down the wet road lit by flashes of emergency lights. Then with my face to the sky I watched the gray clouds race by against a grayer sky, lightning in the distance. No lights out there either. Too black. Walking back toward the van I could see the foundation where the Voths' house had stood. It was illuminated by two errant headlight beams from an upside-down pickup truck in their yard. It had been lifted 30 feet into the air, flipped, then dropped, pinning it between two trees. What about Hillsboro, my family, the Voths' son's family?

Towns look different without street lights, dark, lonely, uninviting. I drove up our drive and ran inside. My family was all right. Thank you Lord.

Now to John Voth's. He was alone at home. How do you tell someone that kind of news? Maybe there shouldn't be an easy way. His family was in Hesston. Several hours went by before we found out they had been spared.

Six months later, during a visit to Harold Voth — living in a mobile home on the site of his old home — I asked him if I could ask a very personal question. Without hesitation his answer was, "sure." "What's the thing you miss most about Ruth being gone?" After one of his thoughtful pauses he said, "Companionship — people don't realize what they've got."

He had to leave to pick up a friend to take to the Senior Center for lunch. Even now, helping others. He moved slowly due to his weakened condition after just over six months of chemotherapy and radiation treatments. Things had not been progressing well. Harold had been in the hospital being diagnosed when the storm took all he had. All except the God he now clung to. Harold often comforted those who came to comfort him.

Four days later, Saturday, September 15 we got the call that told us Harold had gone on. The doctors said it was kidney failure. I think it was the storm.

— Stan Friesen, Nephew of Harold and Ruth Voth

The tornado goes through a dramatic transformation as it leaves Hillsboro as seen in this series of photos from a video taken by Denise Bina.

Meteorologist Jon Davies describes the first photo as the point where the funnel "ropes out" and dissipates just east of Hillsboro. Only minutes earlier, the same funnel had an F5 intensity.

In the second photo the tornado dissipates southwest of Marion Lake, but about 10 minutes and eight miles later, a new one begins forming near Pilsen, as seen in the third photo.

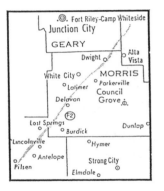

'It's here. It's coming over the top of the Pilsen church.'
— Bob Neuwirth

The March 13 Tornadoes:
Marion County and the North End

After the tornado that had ravaged Hesston an hour earlier passed east of Hillsboro, it lifted and moved through the air above the Marion Reservoir. The twister passed directly over the little town of Pilsen with its St. John Nepomucene Catholic Church, a structure admired for its prairie cathedral architecture. The tornado touched down again beyond Pilsen about five miles northeast of the lake.

For 50 years, Ernest and Agnes Bina had lived about a mile northeast of Pilsen in the house where Ernest grew up. Ernest was terminally ill with cancer; he would die exactly three months after the tornado. The Binas heard tornado warnings, but dismissed them as "just another storm" until their son Raymond called to say the tornado was already at Goessel and they should come to his home one-and-a-half miles from them. Another son, Marion, was at his parents' farm doing chores, but did not go with them. The clouds did not look very threatening there, and he said he would follow as soon as he finished feeding cattle.

"Do you know, we weren't there a half hour when we saw the thing coming toward our place. We saw our place go up, and then we saw the neighbors' go up."

Full of fear, they drove back, not knowing whether or not their son had survived. They were relieved to find him safe in the trench silo with the tractor and feed wagon, but were heartbroken to find their home damaged beyond repair and the outbuildings gone.

The carpets and some of the mattresses were so full

of glass they had to be destroyed. Most possessions were left relatively undamaged, some not even disturbed. On one wall, the Binas had pictures of their children and grandchildren. None was knocked from the wall or broken.

There were, however, some eerie exceptions. "I had two blouses that went out of the closet into the neighbor's pasture," Agnes Bina said. "I just can't figure out how they got out of the closet. Everything else was intact."

Agnes Bina said she was "amazed at how people would pitch in and help and how generous people were." She had special praise for the Red Cross, friends from her church, and the congregation of the Morning Star church northwest of Durham.

The Morning Star church is a member of the Church of God in Christ Mennonite denomination, and their assistance is organized as Christian Disaster Relief. Clayton Wiebe, one of their CDR board members, and his wife Betty estimated helpers from their congregation had worked at least eight days cleaning up behind tornadoes and preparing and serving food.

While working in the Pilsen area, the women from the Mennonite congregation, a group noted for the plainness of their dress and places of worship, served meals in the basement of St. John Nepomucene Catholic Church with its ornate architecture and colorful stained glass windows. Two very different congregations of Christians had come together smoothly in the relief effort.

Robert and Rose Mary Neuwirth saw the Binas'

In the fourth photo the new tornado touches down northeast of Pilsen, and minutes later, as seen in the fifth photo, the twister grows larger as it begins churning debris.

The tornado, with an intensity rating of F2 and winds of about 150 miles per hour, heads northeast toward Lincolnville and Lost Springs in the final photo.

Photos from video by Denise Bina. Assistance in technical descriptions provided by Jon Davies.

house destroyed as they headed for a ditch. "When I was a kid, my dad was terrified of storms," Rose Mary remembered. "We'd have to spend hours down in that stupid cellar with the water in it. I always said . . . when I got away from home, I was never going to spend another minute in a cellar. That day I would have given anything to have a cellar full of water."

When their daughter phoned to say a tornado near Hillsboro was headed in their direction, Bob looked out the window and said, "It's here! It's coming over the top of the Pilsen church."

With no time to seek better shelter, they grabbed jackets and headed for the ditch. "We rounded the house as it took the Bina place. We saw Binas' going up in the air as we turned the corner and ran down and lay in the ditch," Rose Mary said.

Even out in the open, the Neuwirths did not hear the traditional roar, but simply remember the cracking noises as their buildings were broken up. Rose Mary remembers the "hopeless, numb feeling" when the storm had passed and they saw most of their farm buildings swept away and the trees they had planted and carried water to 26 years ago gone. The house stood and was later repaired, but the contents were tossed about and covered with glass and filth.

It took several days for all the farm cats to make their way back, and all but one have died since then. Three females had conceived shortly before the disaster; all had deformed kittens, and two died giving birth.

Among all the rubble in the yard, a little brass swan

was found that the Neuwirths had never seen before. All around central Kansas, debris was showing up at unlikely times and places. It was still sunny and clear at Herington Reservoir when Mark Strand saw a two-by-four splash into the water where he was fishing. Looking up, he saw shingles, insulation, hundreds of popcorn sacks and other junk falling into the lake. When he returned the next day to see what washed ashore, he found a deposit slip bearing the name of a Burrton man and a photograph of a woman and child. He estimated the shower of debris came at least 20 minutes ahead of the storm. It is not unusual in a storm of such length for debris to precede the funnel.

People near Tampa, southwest of Herington, also saw trash fly through the air. Pat Vogt of Tampa remembered that a piece of tablecloth and other bits of debris were falling as the radio reported the tornado was sweeping through Hesston.

The next morning Helen Schwartzman found a piece of a church paper with an address label in her yard east of Tampa. When she heard the television account of Ruth Voth's death, she checked and found it was addressed to Harold and Ruth Voth at Goessel. Ruth had been killed in the tornado. Harold would die six months later of cancer.

According to the *Junction City Daily Union*, checks from the Reimer Plumbing, Heating and Air Conditioning Co. of Hesston were found the next morning near the hospital and the municipal airport in Manhattan, 90 miles to the northeast.

On the living room wall at Selma Pritz's farm home

The St. John Nepomucene Catholic Church in Pilsen is admired by many for its prairie cathedral architecture. The tornado flew over the church's steeple, then touched down again beyond Pilsen. Photo by Jane Vajnar.

On the Selma Pritz farm south of Lost Springs, only one of two silos remains standing in the photo at left. Most of the farm's outbuildings were leveled and the house received considerable damage. Photo by Selma Pritz.
Right: The structure of a machine shed surrounds a combine, tractor and pickup truck on the farm of Robert and Rose Mary Neuwirth farm near Pilsen. Photo by Rose Mary Neuwirth.

'We call it the Hesston tornado that hit Dwight.'
— LoJean Oleen

south of Lost Springs hang two aerial photographs of her farm. One taken several years ago shows a prosperous well-kept farmstead. The other taken in mid-March shows a battered house and piles of rubble where most of the outbuildings had been. Two silos had stood side by side; one was leveled to the ground, while the other remained undamaged.

Corrals were torn up on the next farm, where Pritz's son Maurice lives. The 27 cattle spooked and ran three miles before someone managed to pen them.

Nearby, Mary Haefner's home took some heavy damage, but she was not there. She was in the hospital with severe injuries suffered in a car accident which had killed her husband. As her family cleared away debris, they also prepared for an auction of stock and equipment. She is staying with her daughter in Texas.

The raging funnel missed Herington by a few miles — fortunately, since the city's tornado sirens were not working. The home of Werner and Pauline Monnich southeast of Herington was heavily damaged, forcing them to seek temporary shelter. The Monnichs' two-car garage, a number of outbuildings and half a dozen pieces of farm equipment were destroyed when the twister passed through at 6:40 p.m. The tornado passed near White City, about 12 miles northeast of Herington, tearing up fences and power poles, but no homes were in its path.

But many homes were damaged or destroyed at Dwight in the northeast corner of Morris County, about 25 miles south of Manhattan. Dwight resident LoJean

Oleen recounted a grim community joke: "We call it the Hesston tornado that hit Dwight."

LoJean had supper on the table when her mother called to say there was a tornado on the ground near Parkerville and White City, so she and her teenage children retreated to the family room in the basement. When the radio reported the twister was 18 miles southeast of Junction City, they headed for the adjoining storm cellar.

Jan Oleen, her husband, arrived home just in time to take shelter. When they came back upstairs, the supper was covered with insulation and other trash, and their roof was gone. The winds were followed by rain, resulting in water damage to the eight-year-old house and basement.

Pieces of debris were driven two feet into the ground and had to be pulled out with a tractor.

The day after the storm a friend found the Oleens' dog with her chain caught on a fence post — very frightened, but unhurt. Although the cat disappeared for a week or two, she too returned safely.

The roof of John and Lorna Cronin's home, then nearly new, had been blown off by the tornado that passed through Dwight in 1969; the 1990 storm took the whole house and much of their furniture and possessions.

With its whimsical sort of irony, the tornado blew out a window but did not disturb three tiny plastic deer which were sitting on the sill. Two cedars in the yard grew so close they touched; one was uprooted, and the other remained.

Jan and LoJean Oleen's home south of Dwight stands ripped open and exposed to the elements after the tornado hit their house on the last part of its journey. Photo by Jan Oleen.

The Saturday after the storm was a community cleanup day organized by people from Dwight, Alta Vista and the surrounding area. When the Cronins went to the store for groceries, they were told there was no charge. Money had been donated anonymously to cover the purchases of tornado victims. Workers from the Morning Star church near Durham helped tear down what was left of their house.

"It was a devastating thing," Lorna said, "but there are so many good things that happen to you and so many good people that you almost feel like it was a blessing."

Since the Cronins were adequately insured, they now live in a new, beautifully furnished home on the site of their old one. Yet the Cronins, like hundreds of other storm victims, note that insurance cannot replace the lost family photographs, knickknacks and special gifts from friends they had collected over the years.

Beside the Cronins' new home lies a vacant lot. Until March 13, the Donald Shelton family lived in the house that stood on the lot. The Sheltons pushed the rubble into the foundation, covered it with earth and left. Theirs is one of many places which will be forever altered by the killer tornado which cut a swath more than a hundred miles long through the heart of Kansas.

☐

The Storm

Grandpa's hands shook and his
   eyes filled with tears
As he walked across the farm
   where he had lived for 67 years.
The tornado had dropped swiftly
   out of the sky
And it had destroyed his home
   and he wondered "Why?"

For the past six months he had
   battled cancer for his life
But he had been rescued from this
   storm by his son and his wife
Then he looked around and he
   choked back a cry
"I should have gone with my farm,
   Lord, if I am to die."

His father had built this house
   over a hundred years ago
And he had planted all the trees
   in the large hedge row
Both had been destroyed by a
   tremendous force
And all the fences and power lines
   were broken, of course.

The house was a total loss and the
   buildings were gone
The place looked like it had been
   hit by a bomb.
Large round bales had been
   tossed here and there.
It was just total destruction
   everywhere.

Grandma walked over and took
   hold of Grandpa's hand
As they walked together across
   their land.
It had been their home for almost
   fifty years
It was where their twelve children had
   been born and reared.

It was to this house they had
   come when they first wed
And they had planned to stay
   here forever, they said.
Grandma couldn't bear to start to
   pack
She was hoping against hope,
   they could come back.

"The house is ruined, it's beyond
   repair," the children had said
As their eyes filled with tears and
   their hearts felt dead.
For they had spent every holiday
   together in the living room
They had weathered every storm here,
   shared their happiness and gloom.

It was as though their lives had
   come to an end
They felt too old and tired to start
   over again.
Just then, a rainbow appeared in
   the sky
And the sun peeked out and
   started to shine.

Grandpa heard his grandchildren
   laugh and shout
From then, he had no doubts
We looked at Grandpa and saw
   him smile
It was the first we had seen in
   quite a while.

He patted Grandma's shoulder
   and kissed her cheek
Grandma smiled back at him and
   it made our hearts leap.
"Well, Mom, we've lost almost
   everything here
But I haven't lost the things I
   hold most dear
I've only lost the material things
   in life
I still have my most prized possessions,
   my children and my wife!"

— Harriet Bina

Editor's Note: This poem was written a few weeks after the March 13 tornado by Harriet Bina, the daughter-in-law of Ernest Bina, who died on June 13 of cancer.

The Neufeldt home (at right) was boarded up following the tornado, and the family was forced to move from their longtime home. Photo by Joel Klaassen.

The brick home of Ray and Irma Siemens was totally leveled by the twister. Photo by Irma Siemens.

The March 13 Tornadoes:

In Hesston's Shadow: McPherson County

'*Where did it go? Did it all disintegrate?*'

— Irma Siemens

A mailbox along the McPherson-Burrton road is the only sign the brick home of Ray and Irma Siemens ever existed. Not far away is the boarded-up Kelvin Neufeldt home, eerie against the setting sun. There is no trace of the spacious white barn with a round roof, unlike any other in the county, the pride of generations of Neufeldts.

When Irma Siemens tells of the tornado of March 13, she explains that the site of their home, which is now a cornfield, is a mile south of the "tin pile." This unlikely guidepost was created during cleanup efforts on the corner where the road heads east to Moundridge. The tin pile — a montage of scrap metal from silos, windmills, sheds, irrigation pipe and tractor parts — was all that was left for some of the families hit by the second major tornado to strike Kansas that day.

The tornado started in Harvey County north of Burrton, headed into McPherson County and zigzagged north along County Road 305 — the two-lane blacktop connecting Burrton and McPherson — totally obliterating some homes, sparing others, destroying most keepsakes, leaving a few odd mementos.

Twenty-four-year-old Jeremy Funk had been taking pictures of a rainbow just 15 minutes before the tornado hit. He left his camera upstairs when he saw the twister and ran for the basement. The house was demolished, but the camera was found with lens cap on and film intact.

In anticipation of their second child, Marla and Bret Gillmore were completing the addition of a basement, two bedrooms and a bathroom. As the tornado headed their way just before 7 p.m., Bret, three-year-old Jared and Marla, eight months pregnant, huddled under the stairwell in the recently finished basement. "I remember the noise of the wall breaking and the house falling apart," Marla later recalled.

Hiding in the stairwell had saved them; the tornado left nothing of their home — except the rubble that filled the basement.

Though their home and five outbuildings were totally destroyed, Marla found in the rubble two hand-pieced quilts made by her mother and grandmother. Her wedding dress, packed in a box in an upstairs closet, was intact, and three wedding photos — ripped from the wedding album — were later returned from various parts of the county.

When Irma Siemens emerged from the cellar, she was surprised to see light since the electricity had gone off — and then she realized the house was gone and she was looking up at the sky. All that was left to remind her of her dining table and chairs was a single leg of one chair. There was no sign of china or crystal and the deep freeze was gone — though a frozen turkey and some strawberries were found in the yard. "Where did it go? Did it all disintegrate?" she asked, as she had many times since that turbulent Kansas evening.

Among the wreckage that night Irma Siemens saw a single black scarf dangling from a dresser drawer. "It reminded me of how people used to put a black scarf on the door or mailbox when there was a funeral," she recalled. "That was my funeral," she said of her lost home.

Many area residents were at home that evening, watching television coverage of the tornado that an hour-and-a-half before had struck nearby Hesston, oblivious that another tornado was heading their direction with a vengeance. The families had no warning until the electricity blinked off or unless someone happened to look out a south window and see the quarter-mile-wide funnel on the ground. Each family made it to a basement with seconds to spare and no injuries were reported.

When they emerged, nine families found their homes either totally destroyed or temporarily uninhabitable. Twenty-seven were left homeless and a dozen families had extensive damage to their homes or outbuildings. Damage in McPherson County was estimated at more than $1.3 million, according to figures compiled by Randy Reinecker, director of McPherson County Emergency Management. Damages to the home of Robert and Virginia Friesen and the old Willis school were part of the $24.6 million in total damages for Harvey County, which included the Hesston tornado, according to Lon Buller, director of emergency preparedness for that county.

The tornado is thought to have originated in the sandhills north of Burrton, a few miles south of the Friesen home, one of the first hit. Friesen was on the phone upstairs when he had an eerie feeling and retreated to the basement to be with the rest of his family. "The whole time I've lived in Kansas I've never seen anything like it," he said. "It was big and black and ugly. It's surprising no one was hurt." The Friesens lost their outbuildings, barn, silo, windmill, machinery shed and 18 windows in the house, which was left structurally sound.

From there the twister damaged buildings owned by Arlo Schmidt and Leland Nikkel before totally demolishing the Gillmore house. Moving north at about 30 miles per hour and generating winds up to 200 miles per hour, according to the National Weather Service, the twister mutilated a house Fred and Jan Seiler had just signed a contract to buy. It then ripped apart the Neufeldt home and continued north, destroying farm machinery and metal buildings owned by Don Froese and leaving nothing but a leveled pile of wreckage at the Siemens home. It flattened the home where the Funk family had lived for 19 years and reduced the home of John Thiessen, seven miles east of Inman, to a concrete slab.

Dick Zerger had been checking on his sister in Hesston and was headed home about 7:15 p.m. when he saw the tornado. He sped home to find the upper level of his two-year-old house gone, but his wife and child unharmed in the basement. A lone tree now marks the former homestead of John and Jan Thiessen, nine miles south of McPherson. Several others — including Russell Dick, Sidney Koehn, Alvie Schroeder and Elfriede Stucky — reported damage to their property.

The tornado dissipated a few miles south of McPherson, sparing the most populous town in the county.

Dan Schrag, working his first stint as a volunteer spotter for the National Weather Service that night,

'It was tough to say goodbye to the home place.'

— Kelvin Neufeldt

said there were actually two tornadoes, the one that stayed on the ground the entire time and another short-lived one that did not touch the ground and ran parallel to the major one. He said the twister was on the ground about 20 minutes. Dick Elder, meteorologist for the National Weather Service office in Wichita, said the tornado was on the ground for 15 miles and cut a path about 200 yards wide. It was rated F3 on the Fujita scale, which ranks tornadoes from F0 to F5.

Cleanup started that evening though the sun was fast setting on the mud-encrusted wreckage and downed power lines. The next morning hundreds of volunteers from churches, civic organizations and Inman High School flocked to homes to help owners salvage what they could. Harvey and McPherson counties were both declared disaster areas by Gov. Mike Hayden.

More than a dozen emergency response agencies across the county were called into action during and following the storm, including police departments, emergency medical and ambulance services; the McPherson Amateur Radio Club and county weather spotters; the county sheriff's department and six rural fire districts, according to Reinecker.

While the first home owners reported being hit shortly after 6:45 p.m., the first report did not come into McPherson County sheriff's dispatchers until 6:55 p.m., according to the dispatcher's log. The National Weather Service had issued several tornado watches that day and more than a dozen twisters were sighted. At 4:36 p.m., Reno County had advised of a tornado

'The whole time I've lived in Kansas I've never seen anything like it.'

— Robert Friesen

sighting south of Hutchinson and emergency operations and mobile spotters were dispatched. The sheriff's office was advised that at 4:54 p.m. the severe weather had entered McPherson County. The National Weather Service advised of a second cell of severe weather in western Harvey and northeastern Reno counties, moving toward McPherson County. Mobile spotters sighted a tornado five miles east of Buhler, traveling to the northeast at 6:55 p.m.

Sirens were activated in Inman at 6:55 p.m., but they could not be heard in the rural area devastated by the storm. The sirens were sounded in McPherson at 7:05 p.m. and 7:17 p.m. Reports of damage began to come in at 7:20 p.m., according to the dispatcher's log.

Twenty-nine outbuildings were reported destroyed or unstable, and there was destruction of or extensive damage to dozens of cars, trucks, combines, tractors and farm implements, according to a report compiled by Reinecker. Fifteen head of livestock, valued at $11,000 and uninsured, were lost.

Kelvin Neufeldt had watched the tornado from his dad's house. Driving home he saw the destruction at his neighbors', and was afraid of what he'd find at home. "It was real calm, no air. I didn't know if I'd find my wife alive. The good Lord really watched over us."

After the tornado, the Neufeldt family moved to a trailer on the site of their former home, but could not stand being so close to what Neufeldt called a "dream place" and his boyhood home. They bought some property east of Inman and "will start over, get out of

The seasons at the Gillmore home (left to right): tranquil in winter, devastated in spring, solitary grasslands in summer, and rebuilding in fall 1990. Photos by the Gillmore family and Joel Klaassen.

tornado alley," he said, adding that there have been four tornadoes in that area since 1924 and he'd heard that all four hit on the 13th of the month. "That's four in a hundred years," said the 30-year-old Neufeldt. "That means I could go through two more. It was tough to say good-bye to the home place."

Rosella Funk said her home also was hit in the tornado of 1924. She had been working the night shift on March 13 at Moundridge Manor, a nursing home, and twice had to evacuate the 67 residents from their rooms when tornado sirens sounded just hours apart in Hesston and Moundridge. The Funks planned to rebuild on their five acres in the fall of 1990.

The semi-retired Siemens had not decided what to do as of late summer. "We need a home. I don't know exactly what we'll do," Irma said. "We were semi-retired, now we're completely retired."

Marla Gillmore had a baby girl a month after the tornado. Jared, three at the time of the tornado, remembered the terror for a time. Sometimes when playing with baby Katie he would protect her with a blanket, saying, "Let's play tornado, let's go in the basement."

After the tornado victims pushed away the debris and crawled from their basements that night, they headed for the blacktop, where they were picked up by family and friends. It had been a close-knit community before and though it is even closer now, it likely never again will be the way it was before March 13.

Though the Gillmores planned to rebuild on the same site, it would be without all the antiques Marla had carefully selected for their home and without their longtime neighbors, the Siemens and Neufeldts. "It'll *never* be the same," said Marla. □

'I remember the noise of the house . . . falling apart.'

— Marla Gillmore

53

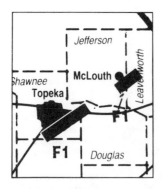

Debris from the Stan and Patty Grewing home litters the landscape on the day after the March 12 tornado, the first twister reported in a rash of tornadoes that struck the state in a 26-hour period over March 12, 13, and 14.

The March 13 Tornadoes:
Topeka Area Funnel Skips Through Suburbs

Like most people in the Topeka area, the Grewings went to sleep on March 12 thinking the worst of the evening's storms were over. But just before midnight, Stan leaped from bed, jolted by what sounded like an explosion.

"I woke up as the house was coming apart," he later recalled. "I was trying to run to the kids' rooms when the house just exploded."

On his way out their bedroom door, he called to his wife, Patty. He couldn't understand why her cries for help sounded so far away. In the split seconds after he jumped from the bed the stone chimney of their walk-out ranch home had come crashing through the ceiling, hitting the bed and carrying it — and his wife — through the floor and into the garage below. If he had not leaped up at that exact instant, he would have been crushed beneath the stones. "It punched a hole in the floor shaped like the bed," he said.

Patty and the waterbed had landed on the car in the garage. She was covered with scrapes and bruises but managed to get back upstairs before Stan could make his way to the lower level. When he opened the door to the baby's room, year-old Sarah was standing up in her crib, clearly visible in the moonlight — the roof had been torn off. Seven-year-old Leslie was still asleep in her room.

By the time the twister struck the Grewings' home southeast of Topeka in the Shawnee Heights area, it had already done major damage to the Shawnee Heights United Methodist Church and the central administration building of Shawnee Heights Unified

> '*I woke up as the house was coming apart.*'
>
> — Stan Grewing

School District 450. The long-tailed twister continued in a northeasterly direction into Jefferson County, where it would damage another church in McLouth before dissipating in Leavenworth County.

Though the Grewings' house was totally destroyed and the loss was estimated at $100,000, Stan said all he felt was elation that his wife and children were okay. "Nothing else in the world mattered," he said. "It changes your priorities pretty quickly." They rebuilt their home in the same location.

In Shawnee County, three homes were destroyed by the twister and 25 were damaged, according to the National Weather Service, which first recorded the twister, which was rated F1, at 11:49 p.m. The path of destruction was about 100 yards wide.

Losses in Shawnee County were estimated at $300,000. Tom Moeller, director of emergency preparedness for Jefferson County, said damages there were less than $100,000.

The deputy who first reported the tornado was in a residential area when it was sighted, so people were not alerted in time to take cover, said Lt. Kermit Crane of the operations division of the Shawnee County sheriff's department. The only way to spot a tornado when it's that dark is during lightning flashes or by the debris, Crane said.

The Rev. Kent Melcher and his wife, Julie, had gone to bed at 11:15 p.m. in the parsonage on the north side of the church, which is about 10 miles southeast of downtown Topeka. They knew there were tornado watches, but the weather didn't seem that bad.

The blasting action of the tornado can be seen in this view of the Grewings' home at 6048 SE 43rd Street in the Shawnee Heights area of Topeka. The Grewings survived without major injuries, even though Patty fell along with her waterbed on the second floor down onto their car in the garage. The twister bounced and skipped across the southeast edge of Topeka, damaging about 25 homes before it lifted. The Grewings' home was a total loss and was later torn down. Photo by Patty Grewing.

About 11:45 Julie sat up in bed and screamed, saying she'd heard an explosion.

The tornado didn't hit the church directly, but went between the church and the parsonage about eight feet off the ground, Melcher said. They think the explosion Julie heard was the tornado ripping the roof off the school administration building warehouse across the street. Most of the damage to the church and parsonage was from flying insulation, tar and debris from the warehouse, Melcher said.

Melcher was walking by the bed when the windows exploded. As he headed downstairs Melcher noticed blood on his foot, which was cut by flying glass. He was taken to the hospital for treatment, and when he returned he was surprised that so many church members had found out so quickly about the damage. About 25 showed up immediately to help and board up windows. Another 25 to 30 showed up the next day to help clean.

Total damage to the church and parsonage was estimated at $40,000. The six damaged stained glass windows were sent to Kansas City to be repaired. Fortunately, the designer and craftsman of the windows still had some of the original glass to mend them.

Across the street at the school district's administration building the roof of the attached warehouse was almost completely torn off by the twister. Surprisingly, there was no damage to the warehouse's contents because there was no rain. "We didn't lose a ream of paper," said Bob Ragan, assistant superintendent for business affairs for the school district. He estimated the damage at between $40,000 and $45,000.

The twister touched down periodically and then lifted over rural areas in southeast Shawnee County as it continued 30 miles northeast to McLouth, a town of 800, where it skipped over house tops almost through the middle of town, a few minutes after midnight.

In McLouth, the twister swooped down on its second church that evening, the white frame Church of the Nazarene, toppling its bell tower. About $40,000 in damage — including $12,000 to have the large stained glass windows repaired — was done to the church, which is more than a hundred years old, said Olin Dalaba, Sunday School superintendent and local barber. The cleanup went well enough that the church was able to hold services that Sunday, he said.

Dalaba had heard the tornado warning on television and waited out the tornado in his basement at home. "The house shook and rattled. I didn't know if we'd make it," he said. "The Lord was watching over me."

As he had almost every morning since coming to McLouth in 1958, Dalaba drove through town to his barbershop the next morning. This time, however, he was startled by what he saw: the church without its belfry, downed power lines, shattered windows and stripped trees. Because there was no electricity the night before, he was not aware of the extent of the damage until that morning.

The date was March 13. Before the sun would set, the city of Hesston and much of central Kansas would lie in ruins, the victim of one of the most destructive tornadoes in Kansas history. □

'That's something to see — a home float away.'
— Roma Boschowitzki

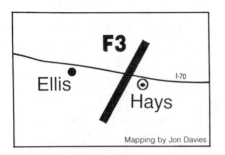

The tornado approaches Bill and Renette Saba while they were trying to flee in their pickup truck. They turned around and rode out the storm at their farm northwest of Hays. The farm received substantial damage from the tornado, which was rated an F3 on the Fujita scale. Photo by Renette Saba.

F3

Ellis • / ⊙ Hays   I-70

Mapping by Jon Davies

The Spring Tornadoes:

Twister Roars Across I-70 In Ellis County

Around 6:30 p.m. on April 25, residents of Ellis County in western Kansas experienced sights and sounds not soon to be forgotten as a menacing black cloud cut a wide swath through more than a dozen farmsteads. Some likened it to a freight train roaring through their homes; others remembered only the sound of shattering glass.

After forming in northern Ness County, the tornado took less than an hour to sweep through Ellis County. By the time it was over, 13 homes would be damaged or destroyed, and dozens of lives would be changed forever.

According to meteorologist Jon Davies, that tornado was one of at least four generated by one thunderstorm that moved from west of Dodge City northeast all the way to Smith Center between 4 and 9 p.m. Though their combined paths on the ground covered nearly 120 miles, and their maximum width was about one-third mile, the tornadoes struck mostly in open country, he reported.

With an intensity rating of F3, the Ellis County tornado was the strongest. It developed near Brownell in Ness County about 5 p.m., cut across the southeast corner of Trego County, then traveled northeast through Ellis County on a path between Hays and Ellis, a farming community 14 miles northwest of Hays and just off Interstate 70.

The David Seibel farm, eight miles south of Ellis, was one of the first and hardest hit. Seibel photographed the tornado that raced through his farm, leaving no building untouched.

"I was sure we were going to get hit," he said later. "I just didn't know how hard."

While Seibel, his wife Verla, and their two daughters hid in the basement and prayed, the twister ripped the roof from their farmhouse, overturned trucks, uprooted trees, and scattered debris across the farm.

When they emerged, Seibel said, "I was surprised there were still some walls left."

An hour after the onslaught, the family stood amid the ruins, hugging each other and crying while friends and neighbors offered comfort. "It's just a terrible feeling," Verla Seibel said.

Five miles southeast of Ellis, Frank and Roma Boschowitzki had just finished feeding their horses when they spied the black cloud looming over a hill near their home. It formed three small funnel clouds and then swirled into one menacing blur of wind and sound.

Frank ran to their home's basement, but Roma, transfixed, watched from the kitchen window as the twister lifted one of her trailer homes into the air and threw it into a field hundreds of feet away.

"That's something to see — a home float away," she said. "I got so hypnotized I didn't move."

She heard the funnel scream past her house, shaking the floor on which she stood. "When it hit the house, it jolted so hard that it shook me," she said. "It scared the life out of me."

Among others whose farms or homes suffered major damage as the storm headed on toward the Saline River Bridge on U.S. 183 Highway were A.E.

INSULATION DEBRIS, covered with snow, layers the hallway in the Jan and LoJean Oleen home, located south of Dwight. The house lost its roof and was pelted by rain following the tornado, and then snow came about a week later. Photo by LoJean Oleen.

THE FRAMED OPEN SKY is displayed in this photo of the kitchen in the Oleen home. The house was rebuilt with the same foundation and frame and was completed in October. Photo by LoJean Oleen.

SECOND TIME AROUND is the appropriate description for the roofless home of John and Lorna Cronin in southeast Dwight. In 1969, the same house lost its roof in another tornado. The 1990 tornado damaged the home beyond repair. Photo by Patricia McDiffett.

PROFILE OF A ROOFLESS barn against the blue sky is seen in this photo of the Robert Neuwirth farm near Lincolnville, about 12 miles northwest of Marion. Photo by Rose Mary Neuwirth.

CLEANING UP THE BACKYARD is the awesome task facing Matthew McDiffett, grandson of John and Lorna Cronin. With the help of friends and relatives, the Cronins were able to build a new house on the same site and move back in on June 7. Photo by Patricia McDiffett.

THE BROKEN HOME of Paul and Rosella Funk projects a lonely profile into the sky on the day after the McPherson County tornado in the photo at left. Stripped of its roof and trashed throughout, the Funk home, six and three-fourths miles east of Inman, is seen before demolition in the middle photo. Setting fire to the remainder of the structure after most of the home was torn down is the final scene in the first act of the rebuilding process for the Paul Funks. Photos by Rosella Funk.

MEMBERS OF THE ZOAR MENNONITE BRETHREN Church (in the photo at left) assist in the cleanup at the Funk farmstead. Photo by Jeremy Funk.

SEARCHING for valuable keepsakes (in the photo at right), Susan Gatz looks up from the basement of the Marla and Bret Gillmore home, located about eight miles west of Moundridge, in this photo taken by her son, Bret Gillmore.

AT THE SIEMENS' FARM (in photo below), six miles east and two-and-and-a-half miles south of Inman, volunteers search for family belongings. Irma's purse and Ray's wristwatch were found intact.

THE SHELLS of two cars remain on the garage floor of what was the Ray and Irma Siemens' home near Inman.

THE ELLIS COUNTY TORNADO

A SQUASHED GRAIN BIN, and an overturned stock trailer which had been thrown 100 yards, litter the landscape at the Edwin Seibel farm six and a half miles south of Ellis. Photo by Terri Seibel.

The ELLIS TORNADO roars across the Kansas plains south of Interstate 70 on April 25. At this point, the tornado is approaching the Dave Seibel farm, seven miles south of Ellis, as seen in this photo taken three miles to the east by Fran Pfannenstiel.

PIECES of a 40-foot by 90-foot machine shed lie jumbled with the Sabas' farm equipment. The tornado uprooted most of the shed's two-foot deep cement foundation and moved it in pieces nearly 50 feet. Photo by Renette Saba.

GOING NOWHERE is this seven-foot by 16-foot gooseneck trailer on the Bill and Renette Saba farm seven miles north and four miles west of Hays. Photo by Renette Saba.

THE BARN AND A MILK HOUSE, which was moved during the storm, stand amidst tons of rubble on the Seibel farm. Photo by Terri Seibel.

A TEDDY BEAR lies ready to be claimed by its owner as the cleanup process begins in this neighborhood in southwest Emporia. Photo by Chuck Frazier.

WHERE TO BEGIN is the question homeowners and volunteers face on June 8, the day after the Emporia tornado. Photo by Chuck Frazier.

CARS SANDWICHED between this Motorcraft truck and the parking lot of North Motors on West Highway 50 in Emporia serve as a reminder to the truck driver of how lucky he was. Minutes before the twister struck, he was persuaded to go inside and let the storm pass. Photo by Chuck Frazier.

THE EMPORIA TORNADO

BROKEN LINES form distorted angles in this view of West 9th Street. Photo by Chuck Frazier.

THE TORNADO is leaving the countryside and entering southwest Emporia about 6:45 p.m. June 7 in this photograph taken eight miles to the south by Eugene Schaeffer, looking north.

THE SEARCH BEGINS for prized possessions at the home of Jim and Joyce Cress at 2420 West View Terrace about one mile from the turnpike in southwest Emporia. The Cresses planned to be in a new home on the site in early 1991. Photo by Chuck Frazier.

GRAIN ELEVATORS at the edge of town provide the backdrop for the remains of the Dan Tebbetts home at 2926 Sutton Place. The Tebbetts lost almost all of their possessions, including their parlor piano seen at the bottom of the photograph. Photo by Aric Kenyon.

TOSSED AROUND LIKE TOYS, cars, debris and the remains of a mobile home lie blended together on the parking lot of the Western Sizzlin Steak House as Joe Pond tries to find out what's left of his car. Photo by Beatrice Pond.

A ROPE OF VIOLENCE scars the cloudy skies in this photo taken by Joanna Kenyon, facing northwest, as the tornado passes through northwest Emporia.

EXPOSED AND TORN OPEN by the narrow funnel as it picked its way through Emporia, the home of Don and Lynne Resch at 2432 West View Terrace stands damaged beyond repair. The house was later leveled and the Resches moved to another location. Photo by Mary Ann Blaufuss.

TORNADO SCULPTURE is seen in this photo by Chuck Frazier of a piece of plywood that sliced into the home of Jim and Diane Anderson at 2634 West Ridge Drive.

VIRTUALLY NOTHING REMAINS of this home in southwest Emporia after the tornado's crossing. Less than 50 yards wide on much of its route, the tornado spared some houses that stood only a few yards from others that were sucked into the air. Photo by Chuck Frazier.

LOREN WAGAMAN walks away from his new home, which was destroyed by the June 7 tornado only two months after being built. Loren and his wife Avanell rebuilt on the same site at 2640 West Ridge Drive and moved into their second new home of 1990 exactly three months after the tornado struck. Photo by Avanell Wagaman.

AN AERIAL VIEW of the Wilbur Janzen farmstead west of Lorraine shows the extensive damage to farm buildings and the century-old farm house, which was moved off its foundation by the May 24 tornado. Photo by Bruce Cates.

SHOVEL IN HAND, Walter Tritsch prepares to tackle the cleanup on his parents' farm, located about two miles north of Bushton. Photo by Max Mehl.

THE MAY 24 TORNADO HEADS toward the Tom Bishop farm west of Durham. This photo was taken by Cheryl Bartel from three miles away, facing north. The Bishop home was totally destroyed.

WITH AN INTENSITY of F3 on the Fujita scale, the tornado packs winds of 200 miles per hour as seen in this photo taken by Dorothy Youk one mile south and five miles west of Durham, facing northwest.

TOSSED ABOUT LIKE STICKS, some of the 87 cars of a Denver-Rio Grande train derailed by the tornado, are seen strewn along the tracks east of Claflin in this photo by Bruce Cates.

THE BIRTH of the March 13 tornado is seen in the top photo by Jon Davies of the supporting mesocyclone cloud formation as it approaches K-17, northeast of Pretty Prairie. The photo was taken at 4:40 p.m., a few minutes after the tornado touched down to begin its 100-mile march.
TWO DAYS BEFORE the Hesston tornado, this tornado is seen as it plows through western Reno County heading into Rice County. The thunderstorm had clouds only 23,000 feet tall, compared to the 35,000 to 55,000 feet height of a typical tornado-producing thunderstorm. The March 11 storm passed near Lyons and Geneseo and produced several tornadoes over its 50-mile route. Photo by Jon Davies.

RENO COUNTY STORMS

ONE-HALF HOUR AFTER the March 13 tornado, salvage work begins on the home of Mick and Edna Astle in southeast Reno County about three miles south of Yoder. The Astles, both in their 70s, safely rode out the tornado in a hallway. Photo by Donald Fischer.

SEARCHING FOR TREASURED FAMILY photos, Connie Brauer sorts through debris on the floor of her home two miles west and a mile north of Haven. The home was rebuilt on the same site. Photo by Sandra Gerhardt.

A 100-FOOT TALL, 37-year-old Silver Maple lies propped against the house of William and Nancy Wilson at 905 W. 20th in Hutchinson after the June 2 storm, one of four wind and hail storms that ravaged Reno County in the spring of 1990. The storms of April 9, June 2, June 7 and June 19 uprooted hundreds of trees and caused more than $30 million in damage, far overshadowing the damage caused by the March 13 tornado in south and east Reno County. The April 9 hailstorm alone produced an estimated $20 million in damage to homes, businesses and cars. Photo by William Wilson.

PAST AND PRESENT are seen in these two photos of what was once the Herman Brauer homestead. Tony Brauer furnished the black and white photo of the house where he grew up north of Haven. The Brauers, who live nearby, sold the farm house to Toby and Wilma Yoder in 1987. The tornado wiped out the Yoders' house, taking even the sub-flooring. Only part of the porch and supporting pillars remain, as seen in this photo by Tony Brauer.

The night of the Ellis tornado, a group of people outside Pleasant Green Assembly of God Church saw a piece of paper flicker in the sky and float to the ground. It was this snapshot of Lacie Bittel and her two dogs. The church, located 12 miles north of Agra, is 80 miles northeast of the home of Dennis and Sharon Bittel, whose mobile home lay in a mass of splintered wood and scraps of metal. Photo by Sharon Bittel.

Slaughter, Marion and Rose Dorzweiler, Audrey Rhyne and Bill Hankins.

The storm also downed power lines and damaged poles, causing power outages in the western half of the county. Midwest Energy, Hays, lost 28 poles and Western Cooperative Electric Association, WaKeeney, lost 40 poles. Most power was restored the next day.

Authorities estimated damage at more than $700,000. Ellis County Sheriff Bruce Hertel said the victims were lucky to be alive. "Some of the homes that were hit were totally demolished," he said. "But most people were warned in plenty of time."

Dennis and Sharon Bittel and their three-year-old daughter Lacie saw television reports of the oncoming tornado and sought shelter at a neighbor's house.

"We were lucky we weren't here," said Sharon Bittel. Their mobile home, nestled into a hill four miles east of Ellis, was a mass of splintered wood and scraps of metal after the storm.

Dennis Bittel surveyed the damage that night, but Sharon waited until the next day.

"That night I tried to cry and I couldn't," she said. "It's almost like it wasn't real to me because I wasn't there to hear the storm."

The next day she was calm but a little dazed as she picked through the rubble. Clothing was scattered here and there, most of it soiled to the point that Sharon wasn't sure whose it was.

Plates, forks and knives were mixed in with mud-covered tumble weeds and insulation torn from the house. Lacie walked through the ruins, screaming with

excitement when she found a toy or familiar object.

A nearby swing set remained untouched, but the things Sharon most wanted — her wedding rings and wedding album — were gone.

A few days later, she got her wish. Friends using a metal detector found the rings, and the company that shot the photographs offered to reprint them for free.

Another treasure that seemed lost forever was found 12 miles north of Agra in Phillips County, 80 miles northeast of the Bittels' home. On the night of the storm, a group of people outside Pleasant Green Assembly of God Church saw a piece of paper flicker in the sky and float to the ground. The paper was a snapshot of Lacie and her two dogs.

Knowing the photograph must have been whisked away from a family during the storm, the churchgoers prayed.

For weeks after the storm, the Bittels received donations of food, dishes, clothes and money. Insurance covered most of the trailer house but few of their belongings.

A fund at the Ellis State Bank helped pay rent for a temporary home in Ellis, and money from the United Methodist Church, the Ellis Knights of Columbus and Hays Kmart employees was used to build a home on the same hill where their trailer was destroyed.

"We've been blessed in a lot of ways," Bittel said. "We've seen the good in people."

Roma Boschowitzki also was touched by the kindness of others. The storm destroyed her garage and several outbuildings. "The wonderful people we met

Dennis and Sharon Bittel's new home is a testimony to the overwhelming generosity of friends and organizations toward tornado survivors. Money from the Ellis United Methodist Church, the Ellis Knights of Columbus, and Hays Kmart employees helped build the house. Photo by Sharon Bittel.

Left: Like a farm toy tossed aside by a child, this old IHC combine rests where it was thrown by the Ellis tornado. Photo by Renetta L. Saba.

Right: Pieces of a puzzle that once made up the David and Anna Seibel farm lie in a jumbled mass on the farmyard six and a half miles south of Ellis. Photo by David Seibel.

'We've seen the good in people. We're overwhelmed by it all.'

— Sharon Bittel

and the love we were shown — that's the thing that brings you through it."

Among those who helped were members of 14 churches, the Knights of Columbus and the Future Farmers of America. A group of Mennonites built fences and hauled away debris.

"They were really something," Boschowitzki said. "You could trust them to operate your machinery and do a good job."

Minutes after the tornado left the county, neighbors arrived at the Seibel farm. They were there for days, picking up tree limbs and junk and hauling it away.

"The response I couldn't believe," Seibel said. "That's done as much for my attitude as anything."

Fred Slaughter, whose farm five miles east of Ellis suffered only minor damage, found truckloads of family possessions in his wheat fields, none of which belonged to him. He found dishwashers, refrigerators, chunks of furniture and bicycles. Most were twisted into pieces and some were unrecognizable.

"The only thing we found in one piece is a shoe," he said. "Now we have to find the other one."

Roma Boschowitzki said she and her husband cleaned up most of the mess in a few months, but not without a struggle.

"I never worked so hard in my life as I did this year," she said. "I'm glad we lived through it, but it wasn't easy."

While most of the Boschowitzkis' belongings were insured, much of their farm equipment was not. They lost $30,000 in machinery and were forced to hire a

custom cutter to harvest their wheat because their combine was destroyed.

If the cleanup was long and arduous, rebuilding was even more so.

The Seibels rented a home in Ellis, leaving behind what was left of their farmhouse. They would rebuild some day, Seibel said, but he decided it would be easier to stay in town for a while.

"It might be better," he said. "I don't have to look at the mess in the evenings. I get depressed if I spend too much time out here."

Nearly five months after the storm, his shelter belt was still littered with broken trees, and all but one outbuilding stood unrepaired. Seibel said it probably would be years before his farm was back to normal.

Ironically, the tornado helped the Bittels realize a dream. Dennis broke his hip two weeks before the storm, and the Bittels had to delay building a new house. After their trailer and possessions were destroyed, they decided to build from scratch rather than try to salvage what little remained.

"It was easier to have everything gone than to have to pick up the pieces," Sharon Bittel said. "The Lord gave us a fresh start."

Their new start brought good fortune; Dennis' hip healed, and Sharon gave birth to their second child, Logan Joseph. "God has taken some things away," Sharon said. "But he's given so much back to us." □

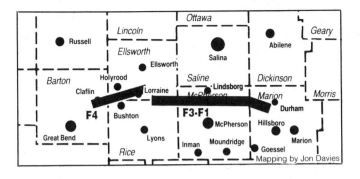

Mapping by Jon Davies

Eighty-year-old Ida Gasaway took a brief flight when the tornado lifted her up and deposited her outside. Ida survived with some broken bones, bruises, and a sprained ankle. The home, as seen above, was destroyed. Photo provided by Ida Gasaway.

The Spring Tornadoes:
Twisters Strike Central Kansas on May 24

Just before suppertime on May 24, a huge storm was brewing along Kansas Highway 4 in Barton County. In the next few hours the storm would spawn more than half a dozen tornadoes, which would wreak havoc in at least six central Kansas counties, causing millions of dollars in damage and destroying 40 farmsteads.

The first official report by the National Weather Service at Concordia of the funnel touching down came at 4:10 p.m. when it was sighted two miles northwest of Hoisington. From there it headed almost straight east, gathering strength that peaked at nearly the same intensity as the tornado that devastated Hesston on March 13.

From Barton County, the tornado cut a swath along the Ellsworth-Rice county line before entering into McPherson County. The last sightings were in Marion and Chase counties as late as 10 p.m.

In all, the tornadoes, whose path was close to 100 miles long, caused from $4 million to $6 million in damage. While dozens of farms and homes were damaged that evening, there were no large towns in the tornadoes' path so the damage was relatively low compared to the March 13 twisters.

There were no fatalities but several injuries were reported, including an elderly Claflin woman and four oil field workers, who were among the first hit, according to the National Weather Service. Ida Gasaway, 80, hid in a closet while her home four miles east and a half mile south of Claflin collapsed around her. Four oil field workers were servicing a rig north of Bushton

when they spotted the tornado and decided to outrun it. Rescue workers had to cut the men from the car and they were hospitalized briefly.

Ida Gasaway, who suffered two broken bones in her foot, recalled: "I got down on my hands and knees, and I had two heavy afghans I'd crocheted and I put those over the top of me. And that's the last I remember. I didn't know anything until I was airborne . . . and I thought, 'Well, this is it.' . . . I don't know whether something hit me or not, I did have a big bruise on my head. But I really didn't know anything until I came to. I didn't know when it let me down."

She found herself outside what had been her house, debris still flying past her. The carpeting was ripped off the floors, a bathtub was found half a mile away and the refrigerator was never found at all. Friends and strangers, including a group from Mennonite Disaster Services, arrived almost immediately to help with cleanup. One found her pocketbook with nearly $500 in it and many fragile knickknacks were also found intact.

Six months later, Gasaway, who had moved into a house in Claflin, said she had "healed up pretty well" from her injuries, which included broken bones in a toe, a sprained ankle, and "black and blue" bruises on her head, shins and legs. She had never been in a tornado before, she said, and "I sure don't care to be in another."

About a half mile from Gasaway's farm, the tornado — spawning winds more than 200 miles per hour at times — derailed 87 of 103 cars of a Denver-Rio

'Well, this is it.'

— Ida Gasaway

Debbie Urban didn't used to believe in getting into a ditch if caught in a vehicle during a tornado. But after she and her husband Mike endured the May 24 tornado from the vantage point of a ditch, she's a believer. The two pickups they abandoned ended up half a mile away. Photo of the Urbans by Jane Vajnar. Photo of truck by Mike Urban

> **'I was running, but I wasn't touching the ground.'**
>
> — Debbie Urban

Grande train. At the time of the storm, the freight train was rolling westward between Bushton and Claflin. As the storm — which they did not realize was a tornado — approached, T.R. Adams, the conductor, turned to Chuck Koepke, the engineer, and asked him, "If there is a tornado in there, do you think it could blow these engines over?"

Koepke confidently replied, "No, I don't think so."

But when the wind became strong enough to slow the train's speed, they decided to stop and go to the inner cab of the engine to wait out the storm. They heard flying debris hitting the locomotive and felt the engine rocking. Both engines remained upright — as did the 16 rear cars and the caboose containing the other crew member — but 87 cars at the front of the train were jumbled like a train set abandoned by a careless child.

East of Claflin, Mike and Debbie Urban were mowing a cemetery in preparation for Memorial Day. As the clouds grew more ominous, they decided to head back to town. They had two pickups at the cemetery and each started driving one back to Claflin. The winds grew more fierce and they continued to drive — until Debbie saw the electric poles next to the road snapping off and Mike saw "these big old oak trees . . . the wind just sucked them up to a peak, and then they just exploded."

Mike decided to stop and head for a ditch and Debbie followed his lead. As they were trying to get out of the pickups, the wind tore the doors from their hands and sucked Debbie from the cab. "I was airborne," she

remembered. "I was running, but I wasn't touching the ground." Mike watched his pickup, which was in park, roll down the road and heard a window break out of the truck and his wife scream.

"I couldn't talk for a week or two afterward," Debbie said, "because I'd lost my voice from screaming."

Sand and trash driven by the merciless winds cut through their clothes. In trying to reach Debbie, Mike blacked out, but when he regained consciousness, he was shielding Debbie's body with his own.

As they lay in the ditch 16 to 18 inches deep, everything imaginable flew over them — including a deer four to five feet off the ground. Debbie said she had not previously believed in advice to get out of your car in case of tornado. "I thought, 'there's no way I'm getting out of my vehicle and getting into a ditch,' " she said. "Hey, I was glad to be there. And it works."

When the storm had passed, Debbie realized Mike had been enduring the "sandblasting" on his naked back. "Oh, Mike!" she exclaimed. "You didn't even have a shirt on."

His reply was, "I did when I got out of the pickup." His T-shirt was tied in a knot around his wrist, where it had caught on his watch as the wind sucked it from his body.

They suffered abrasions from the "sandblasting" as well as Debbie breaking a finger and Mike's eyes being scarred. Their pickups ended up half a mile down the road.

From there the funnel headed east to Bushton where it destroyed a barn housing 36 sows owned by

Ida Gasaway cradles one of her fragile knickknacks which survived the tornado. Photo by Jane Vajnar.

Looming ominously over Bushton, the tornado threatened the town but didn't invade it. Photo by Jay Huebner.

Agnes Bina and her husband Ernest lost their home near Pilsen in the March 13 tornado. On May 24, their son Dean and his wife Pat had their own tornado experience just a few miles away. On June 13, her husband died of cancer. Photo by Jane Vajnar.

Maurice and Betty Dohrman and their son and daughter-in-law, Jeff and Denise Dohrman. None of the sows or their litters were harmed though the barn collapsed around them.

Don and Marie Schepmann, who owned a swine operation between Bushton and Holyrood, were not so lucky. At least 20 of their hogs were either killed in the storm or later destroyed. Their barn was reduced to splinters, most of the granary was blown away, and their hog sheds, garage and machine shed were completely obliterated. Their horses were seriously injured and their cattle — spooked by either the storm or cleanup efforts — were found as far as 16 miles away.

Three miles south of Holyrood, which is north of Claflin and Bushton, the Frees home was ripped off its foundation as Karma Frees and her three children — Jayme, Bradley and Kari — huddled in the basement under a stairway with four pillows and a flashlight.

"The first big sound I remember was the stairs," Karma said. "We're sitting under the stairs and I heard this big creaking, and the stairs just went, just rose up. I could see them leave, and at that point the kids started screaming. I thought we were gone at that point. My first thought was trying to run. I rose up and could see stuff flying all around us and I went right back down and just kept over (the children) and kept talking to them, trying to keep them calm. They were great."

Furniture from the basement was flying past and three of their four pillows were sucked away from them. She tried to grab some of the objects flying past to use for protection and a mattress was ripped from her hands. At last she managed to grab the end of a baby crib and hold it over the children through the rest of the storm.

When Jim Frees realized the tornado was heading near his home, he left his job at the Enron gas plant. He saw a funnel on his way home and finally became frightened enough to stop and wait out the storm in a neighbor's yard. When he arrived home, "The only thing sitting there was the car."

All that was left of the house, garage and an old granary — a local landmark — was a piece of garage wall smashed up against the car. All the three-fourth inch rock had even been blasted off the driveway, a phenomenon noticed by other tornado victims.

He found his wife and children sopping wet and covered with mud, but essentially unhurt except for a bump on Karma's head and surface cuts. They received donations of furniture and clothing from people in the community and when Jim's company published information about the disaster in its bulletin, cash donations came from company employees as far away as Louisiana and Texas.

Don and DelJean Nash and their two sons live just down the hill from the Frees' home. DelJean was just starting to take the boys to swimming lessons, but turned back when she saw the dark clouds.

They went to the basement and DelJean put a box spring against the wall and got under it, encouraging the children to "practice" what they would do if a tornado came. They heard a shrill whistling sound and

Far Right: Teamwork and to-getherness rebuilt the Dohrmans' hog facility, as it did many other structures following the storms in Kansas this year. Photo by Joy Hoelscher.

Right: The wind huffed and puffed and blew this hog barn down, but none of the sows or pigs inside were hurt, according to owners Maurice and Betty Dohrman and Jeff and Denise Dohrman of rural Bushton. Photo by Betty Dohrman.

'All I have left in those boxes are broken memories.'

— Delmar Wesseler

the sound of the house breaking apart. "It was just a horrible, horrible roar with grinding and crunching, and I thought it was never going to quit," she said.

They had lost one home to chinook winds in Alaska and their mostly brick two-story house — which they built themselves — was especially strong. "We had hurricane straps. Rafter tiedowns. We took a lot of preventive measures," said Don, who was away at a convention during the storm.

But even those measures could not withstand the storm's force. The house remained standing but had to be torn down. The top floor was tilted in one direction and the bottom in another.

Ironically, Don and DelJean had gone to Hesston in March and signed up with Mennonite Disaster Services to aid in the cleanup effort. Now MDS returned their help.

The Nashes were able to save most of their personal possessions, but the salvage operation itself was an ordeal. Three months after the tornado, DelJean said that everything she touched either cut her, made her itch, smelled bad or all three. Many of her clothes were still in her closet, but covered with insulation, glass and even pieces of shingles from the roof.

Milton and Dorothy Tritsch, who were getting their house near Holyrood in shape for their retirement, waited out the storm in their basement. They lost outbuildings and three cows and their house was declared a total loss by the insurance company. Their dog, Cocoa, who was afraid of storms and who refused to leave the machine shed, survived. So did the cat and

her newborn kittens in the demolished barn, though she later fretfully would continually move her kittens as if looking for a safe haven. One of their memories is of the loud chatter of the birds, eager to build new nests. The Tritsches moved to a house in Holyrood following the storm.

The twister continued east toward Lorraine and the home of Delmar Wesseler, whose wife had died the week before of cancer. His mother had died just months earlier, and he and his sons had gone to the Indianapolis 500 over the long Memorial Day weekend in an attempt to lift their spirits.

They were near Santa Claus, Indiana, when they saw a television news report of a tornado in the vicinity of Great Bend and Hoisington. They called a friend at home and heard the shocking news that everything at their home was gone.

Fearing what they'd find, they sped home. All the outbuildings had been reduced to piles of rubble, and farm machinery in the sheds was a total loss. The top part of the house was gone and the rest damaged beyond repair. Neighbors helped salvage what they could, boxing up what little remained.

"All I have left in those boxes are broken memories," Delmar said.

The 1880s house and a big barn that were demolished had been built by Delmar's great-great grandfather, who came to the farm in 1872. "We don't even have an identity," Delmar said.

While his sons recovered their Baylor University rings and Delmar found his wife's Bible, they could not

Far left: Evidence of the tornado's fury can be seen in this photo by Gary Unruh. The twister, which still had winds approaching 100 miles per hour as it approached Durham, left the Tom and Helen Bishop modular home in shambles.

Scrambled, diced and spliced is one way of describing the tornado-processed remains of the farm of Andrew, Vernon and Elma David west of Durham. Photo by Rev. Lloyd Harsch

find a videotape of the Wesselers' 40th anniversary celebration.

One of Wesseler's checks landed on a window sill some 70 miles away. The woman who found it sent it back with $25 and a note. "Something bad must have happened to you. I hope this helps," it read.

Delmar Wesseler could have let any of the recent tragedies crush him, but he persevered in bringing order out of the chaos and began making plans for the future. Despite his own adversity, he, more than anyone else, kept a census of the people from the Mennonite Disaster Service and other neighbors and strangers who assisted at his farm. He said there were more than 200 workers from 29 churches on Memorial Day alone. By early August helpers had put in 6,000 hours of work there. To repay their efforts, he planned to go to the Mennonite Central Committee auction next spring and buy a quilt.

Just outside of Lorraine the tornado bore down on the farm of Randle and Vada Rolfs.

When the Rolfs, both 80, emerged from their basement, they found havoc. All the outbuildings — a barn, granary, machine shed and bunkhouse — were demolished. In one room of the house, ceiling tile littered the floor, and insulation hung in shreds. Seventy panes of window glass were broken. Small objects had been sucked out of the house and pulled in from outside. There were milo stalks under the beds. Vada described the filthy rooms as looking as if someone had hurled buckets of muddy water at the walls.

Yet, here as everywhere, the tornado's power was selective. Vada had been working on plans for her Bible school class in the dining room. Though debris littered the house, the materials still lay in five neat stacks for each day of the week.

There were reports of that tornado dissipating near Lorraine, but that one or another soon reappeared, resuming its destructive path south of Marquette where it tore up several farms along the "river road" between Marquette and Lindsborg in McPherson County. Tornado sirens in Marquette warned residents of the tornado's approach at 6:12 p.m. when the funnel was sighted four miles southwest of town. After the tornado had passed Lindsborg shortly after 6:30 p.m., Carl and Edna Oakleaf emerged from the basement of their home southwest of Lindsborg to find a flattened silo, chicken house and cattle shed. Their neighbors, the Cranes, lost their mobile home.

Continuing eastward on a path three miles south of Roxbury, the twister then tore a wing off the barn and destroyed the outbuildings of Robert and Marilyn Geis, who also lost many large trees. Even more trees were uprooted at the next place east, one owned by Andrew, Vernon and Elma David.

Elma and Andrew sought shelter in an underground pumphouse. (Vernon, their brother, was not at home.) As the tornado neared, they put their hands over their ears. "You could feel the vacuum," Andrew said. "Other people might call it pressure, but it is actually a vacuum. It makes your hair stand on end."

After the twister passed, they found the machine

A brace holds up one wall so Milton and Dorothy Tritsch can occupy their home temporarily after the May 24 tornado. The house was later leveled and the Tritsches found a home in Holyrood. Photo by Jane Vajnar.

Carl and Edna Oakleaf emerged from their home southwest of Lindsborg to find a flattened silo, cattle shed and chicken house. Photo by Jane Vajnar.

This aerial view of the Delmar Wesseler farm near Lorraine shows the damage that winds from an F4 tornado can do. Photo by Bruce Cates. Below, a close up look at the Wesseler farm after it was ravaged by the May 24 tornado. Photo by Irvin Harms.

shed and other outbuildings reduced to rubble and the lane completely clogged with trees. The house was off its foundation but nearly intact.

Several rows of 30- to 40-foot cedars north and west of the house, another row of cedars along the lane road and some ashes and Chinese elms were all uprooted like radishes. "None of us are going to live long enough to grow trees that big again," Elma David said.

When Tom and Helen Bishop returned to their home west of Durham, they found their belongings literally gone with the wind and their home totally destroyed.

Helen, as might be expected, was anguished the most by those items which could not be replaced — souvenirs from her childhood and keepsakes relatives had brought from Prussia to her grandparents.

Continuing its almost straight easterly path, the tornado passed north of Marion Lake, then ravaged the farm of Dean and Pat Bina east of Pilsen, only a few miles from another home that had been destroyed in the March 13 tornado — the home of Ernest and Agnes Bina, Dean's parents. At Dean and Pat Binas', the twister demolished outbuildings and uprooted trees in a complete circle around the house, which received only minor damage. The Binas and their son Jeff took refuge in a windowless bathroom in the center of the house. Suddenly Dean realized Pat was missing, but she soon returned — carrying her rosary. Minutes later, the tornadic storm had passed and dissipated as it moved east into Chase County. ☐

As the eyes of Eugene Schaefer and his camera witness the violence eight miles to the south, the tornado sets its sights on Emporia.

Friends of Loren and Avanell Wagaman, 2640 West Ridge Drive in Emporia, gather after the tornado left its destructive mark on the Wagaman home. Photo by Avanell Wagaman.

The Spring Tornadoes:
A Rope of Violence Scars Emporia

On June 7, a severe storm cell several miles south-southwest of Emporia spawned a family of tornadoes as it moved north. Four of them touched ground, and one snaked its way into the city.

The slender funnel, sometimes looping around itself, stretched like a rope across the northwest edge of the city and randomly struck business and residential areas. Sirens alerted residents to take cover, but two people received serious injuries in the storm, and another 19 were treated at local hospitals for minor injuries.

The tornado entered town about 6:45 p.m., first striking south of Sixth Avenue in west Emporia, where it demolished several businesses and houses and caused its most serious injuries.

Doug Main, 24, with his three-month-old daughter Maizie, had driven to his brother's house to seek shelter in the basement.

"I could see the tornado coming from the south as I drove up," Main said. Clutching the baby in an infant carrier, he ran toward the house. As he reached the door, the tornado pulled Maizie from his arms, then sucked Main into the air.

"I lost all control of where I was going," he recalled. "The next thing I knew I was upside down. I landed on my head on the cement by my brother's garage.

"When I first regained consciousness, I couldn't move any part of my body. My arms and legs were numb. I thought I was paralyzed."

His brother Ed helped him while others began to search for Maizie. They found her, unconscious and still strapped in the infant carrier, in the tall grass of a vacant lot about 30 feet away from the house. The tornado also had picked up Ed Main's pickup, which had been parked directly in front of Doug Main's car; Ed's truck had been dumped in the lot next to the baby.

Both victims were taken to Newman Hospital, where they waited almost five hours before they could be moved to another hospital for treatment. An unrelenting downpour grounded a hospital-service helicopter, and the pair eventually were taken by land ambulance to Stormont-Vail Regional Medical Center in Topeka.

Doug Main lay face-up and completely immobilized at the Emporia hospital. A tube had been inserted into his mouth to his stomach to prevent him from vomiting and, perhaps, killing himself. Sometimes the swelling in his throat almost shut off his ability to breathe.

"At one point in time, I thought I was going to die," Main said. "I knew I was hurt badly. They were over there asking if they should call a priest."

"For the last rites," explained his wife, Imelda, 21. "We're Catholic."

Imelda Main had arrived at the Emporia hospital to find her husband lying in a pool of blood. Their daughter was in an adjoining room with several broken bones in her right arm, internal injuries and severe cuts.

"I think the only reason she survived was because of her (infant) seat," Imelda Main said. "She had

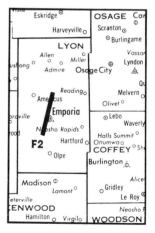

Stripped of its dignity and open to the elements, this house on the west side of Emporia received major damage from the June 7 tornado. Photo by Mary Ann Blaufuss.

Dozens of new and used vehicles at John North Ford in Emporia met an untimely demise before leaving the dealer's lot. Photo by Aric Kenyon.

In a southwest Emporia neighborhood, a house displays an unusual twist of a venetian blind, thanks to an unusual twist of nature. Photo by Chuck Frazier.

bruises all over her."

Main suffered two broken vertebrae in his neck and one in his back. Plastic surgeons repaired his cheek, which had been cut to the bone in the incident. Orthopedists installed a "halo" device to keep his head immobile for at least three months. Attached to a sheepskin-lined vest around his torso, the halo was held in place by metal guides and four screws that pierced his flesh to the skull. When the screws loosened, as they periodically did, the pain was almost excruciating, he said.

The halo was replaced after three months with a cervical collar, which Main would wear at least until early 1991. Then, perhaps, he would be released to return to work, trimming chuck roast on the line at IBP beef-processing plant.

"Eventually, it'll be completely healed, but it'll take a long time," he said.

Across the street from Ed and Lisa Main, Dan and Jennell Tebbetts and their dog had taken shelter in a concrete closet in the basement of their home. Their two children and two foster children were out of town when the tornado struck.

"We never heard anything breaking or falling in the house," Jennell Tebbetts said. "We felt the house shake, and then the wall fell in on my husband. It felt like we were falling in very, very slow motion. I looked down at my arm and I saw my watch flying through the air."

Dan Tebbetts, who had covered his wife's body

with his own, tunneled through the debris and brought them both to the surface.

"We thought we'd go upstairs and the roof would be gone. When we got outside and turned around to look at our house, there was no house," she remembered.

"That was the biggest shock of all. There was nothing but rubble. There were no whole pieces of anything — no clothes, no shoes, no little things. You know, things you take for granted. Like you go to a bathroom and have a toothbrush. You could sit around and cry, but it wouldn't accomplish anything, it'd just depress you."

She escaped with scratches, but her badly cut and bruised husband required 10 stitches to close one of his wounds. The dog also was injured.

The couple was grateful to be alive and grateful, too, for friends and strangers who rallied to help.

The owner of a sporting-goods store donated about $400 worth of clothing to the family; others searched for and found missing items, including old income-tax returns and the family's parakeet, which was still alive.

Photographs scattered blocks away were returned and later refurbished by a local photographer. Among the photos was a portrait of Jennell Tebbetts' late great-grandparents.

"I thought, 'If I find nothing else, I want that picture,'" she said, "and someone, through the rubble, looked and found those pictures. I don't know how we'll ever get across how grateful we really are."

The Tebbetts family moved early in September to a

Tornadic Tricks

Few forces in nature can pull the strange, uncanny tricks that a tornado performs on a regular basis. For a twister, it is second nature to stab objects into each other, wrap metal around wood, bend and snap poles, and obliterate one item while giving reprieve to something right next to it. These photos by Chuck Frazier depict a few tornadic tricks.

Residents of Emporia Learned Lesson from Tornado That Terrorized City 16 Years Earlier

When the west side of Emporia was hit on June 7, hundreds of Emporia residents did a double take: They had seen the face of a tornado before, almost 16 years ago to the day, on June 8, 1974. And that tornado had hit the west side of town.

But before the 1974 tornado, many Emporia residents believed the town was tornado-proof. Any town situated between two rivers could not be struck by a tornado, they had been told, and Emporia was nestled between the Cottonwood River on the west and the Neosho River on the east.

The theory was as widely accepted as any Old Wives' Tale. But the June 8, 1974 tornado proved the Old Wives had lied. On that day, a massive funnel formed on the west edge of town and swept down within minutes on the Flint Hills Mall Shopping Center. Leaving the mall almost destroyed, it cut a wide swath of destruction through an apartment complex, a residential area, and on to a trailer park. Sirens had sounded eventually, but for many the warning was too late.

When the 1974 tornado finally lifted, seven people were dead, 80 were hospitalized, and scores of others had minor injuries.

Rescue and clean-up work was chaotic. Leaders had not prepared themselves or the town's 25,000 residents to cope with the aftermath of a tornado. They learned quickly.

Within a few years, a group of volunteers, law-enforcement officers and emergency personnel had been organized into an efficient Emergency Preparedness group. When the next tornado struck Emporia in 1990, residents of this east-central Kansas city were much better prepared.

house they bought a mile or so north of the site where their old house had stood.

The tornado moved from Sixth Avenue north along Graham Street and continued across Highway 50. Tim North, owner of John North Ford, watched from a restaurant window in a mall a few blocks away as the tornado inflicted nearly $1 million in damages to cars at his dealership.

The tornado demolished 31 new vehicles and 40 to 45 used ones; 240 other new and used units also were damaged, but insurance covered most of the losses, North said.

Emporia police officer Mark Locke, near the car lot, watched as the tornado flattened Norton Oil Company, where employees hid safely in a rear restroom. The tornado crossed the highway and struck the car lot before destroying Emporia Rental Center to the east.

Officer Locke reported that a pickup truck was turning into the front drive of the car lot when the tornado hit.

"It picked him up, spun him around and threw him in the back lot," Locke said. The driver suffered a shoulder injury and cuts. "His truck was still driveable."

From Highway 50, the tornado jogged slightly northeast a few blocks, damaging rooftops as it spun, until it reached the DeBauge Brothers Coors/Coca-Cola distributorships. Workers on night duty found safety in a restroom while one building's pre-stressed concrete walls crumbled under the force of the tornado.

About 200 yards from the distributorship,

> **'I watched this housing district explode.'**
> — Undersheriff Randy Thomas

firefighters at Station Two hid in a floor pit in the station garage as the tornado passed. They speculated that the storm would strike next at the Dolly Madison bakery about a block north. The firefighters, who also are emergency-medical technicians, ran toward the bakery to help, but the twister skipped over the plant, narrowly missed the high school, and headed toward the West Ridge residential area.

The twister's course was almost parallel to and only a few blocks west of Industrial, a major business thoroughfare that was hit by the tornado that struck Emporia in 1974. A slight deviation in the storm's path would have caused millions of dollars more in damages.

Lyon County Undersheriff Randy Thomas followed the tornado from the highway as it headed north.

"I watched this housing district explode," Thomas said. "I was about two blocks behind it."

He said the twister was "almost running at a 45-degree angle from the bottom to the base. It tied itself in a knot."

The whirling winds picked up a semi-trailer truck on the nearby Kansas Turnpike and deposited the trailer across Graphic Arts Road at the west side of the housing development. The cab of the truck was left overturned in a ditch by the turnpike. The driver was admitted to Newman Hospital and released the next day.

In West Ridge, the tornado worked the eerie wonders characteristic of its breed.

The twister demolished the home of Jim and Joyce

The morning after the storm claimed the home of Dan and Janelle Tebbetts, Dan sits in a lawn chair that survived the storm and discusses the tragedy with friends and neighbors. Photo by Aric Kenyon.

Undaunted by steep roofs or other physical challenges, and with their hearts set on recovery rather than the seemingly endless destruction, workers like these on the roof of the Chuck Grimwood home in Emporia brought hope to the survivors. Photo by Chuck Frazier.

Cress, but left untouched a gun cabinet, and a kitchen table and chairs. Joyce Cress said the guns in the cabinet were intact and a key hidden on top of the cabinet had not moved at all.

Les and Joyce David's house also was destroyed, but the glass from a coffee table was not damaged; the table itself was in slivers.

The roof of a two-year-old house owned by Mike and Becky Carlson was lifted from the house, then set back down. The garage and one end of the house were reduced to sticks of wood.

Most of those affected decided to repair or rebuild. A few residents whose homes were destroyed bought other houses.

The tornado that struck Emporia was one of at least nine tornadoes in Kansas that night, according to meteorologist Jon Davies. None of the twisters was more than 100 yards wide, and none had a path longer than 10 miles. The Emporia tornado was the most destructive.

According to a report compiled by local, state and federal officials, 30 businesses were struck by the tornado and five sustained major damage. Of the 34 homes affected, 12 were destroyed, three had major damage and 19 had minor damage. Most of the homes were in an affluent neighborhood and were thoroughly insured.

Gov. Mike Hayden declared Lyon County a disaster area two days after the storm struck, but federal officials withheld the designation.

The total damage estimate was reported at $5.6 million by Emergency Preparedness Director Steven Davis, an Emporia attorney.

Davis arranged for a Small Business Administration official to provide low-interest loan applications to Emporians whose insurance was not adequate to cover losses. He added that response to the emergency "went unbelievably well. I just don't think it could have gone any better."

Volunteers, law officers, emergency and medical personnel and National Guard troops came almost immediately to the command post set up at Station Two.

Davis and Police Chief Larry Blomenkamp agreed that while some of the logistics would be changed for future emergencies, the overall response plan had worked.

Davis also praised the response from the Mennonite Disaster Service.

"Bless their hearts, those people quietly come into town and go about their business," he said. "Their assistance is priceless. How do you say thank you to those people? They're not there for the thanks."

The Mennonites brought their own heavy equipment to the area, asked where they could be used, and went to work. They were "unbelievable," Davis said. "These people, when they come in, they even bring their own food! They are no burden to anyone. They just help." □

'These people, when they come in, even bring their own food.'

— Steven Davis

Lance Vanley holds the ladder for Ted Mayes as he undertakes tree repair work after the June 19 wind storm. The Lance and Julia Vanley residence in the town of Sedgwick on the Sedgwick-Harvey county line was one of thousands with tree damage in a six-county area. Photo by Vanessa Mayes.

Only a skeleton remains of this hangar at Jabara Airport in northeast Wichita after it was destroyed by the 100-mile-per-hour winds on June 19. Photo by Dave Dinell.

Wind, Hail and Rain Storms:
Rare Inland Hurricane Blasts Wichita Area

On Tuesday night, June 19, a wind storm swept from southwest to south-central Kansas, leaving behind property damage estimated at $50 million, twice as high as damage estimates from the March 13 tornadoes. Meteorologists called the storm system — which bred a wind shear storm or "inland hurricane" — one of the worst of the century.

The six-hour storm intensified near Pratt about 8:15 p.m., and winds reached speeds ranging from 65 to 120 miles per hour as the system moved east and slightly north through parts of six counties. According to Joe Rosner of the National Weather Service, wind speeds of 75 miles per hour are considered hurricane force.

From Pratt, where the wind was clocked at 65 miles per hour and carried three-quarter inch hail, the gathering storm moved east to Kingman where 100 mile-per-hour winds uprooted trees, downed power lines and devastated roofs. Traveling northeast, the storm blew across Cheney Reservoir and Reno County into western Sedgwick County shortly after 9 p.m. (See page 100 for more details on Reno County.) By 9:45 the storm had buffeted Wichita, left nearly 20,000 homes without power, and knocked out most of its radio and television stations. By 10:15 it was sweeping into parts of Butler and Harvey counties.

Confirmed tornado sightings were made in Sedgwick, north of Haven and near Bentley, according to Rosner. Sightings also reportedly occurred near Andale, Halstead, Whitewater, Hutchinson, Nickerson and west of Valley Center. The storm was so intense

that it continued to create wind speeds of 80 miles per hour in northeast Kansas two hours after leaving the Wichita area, he said.

A second wave of storms packing 85 mile-per-hour winds passed through Sedgwick, Harvey, Butler and Reno counties between 12:30 and 1:30 a.m.

"It was a real humdinger," Rosner said of the storm. "It was off all our readings. The top of it was 70,000 feet high. We couldn't get it on our readings."

In Wichita, sirens sounded three times during the night, and wind speeds were estimated at more than 100 miles per hour. Houses shifted on their foundations. Mobile homes blew away. Glass shattered, and hundred-year-old trees toppled. More than a thousand utility poles were snapped, leaving many power lines dangling in the wind. Large and small vehicles alike were blown into ditches.

Wichita Camp Fire Girls campers ran for cover as trees fell onto their tents. Baseball fans at Lawrence-Dumont Stadium either left as soon as the siren atop one of the stadium light poles sounded or took cover in restrooms and coolers. All bets were off as the wind raced through Wichita Greyhound Park, leaving a trail of glass shards.

About 60,000 KG&E customers across six counties were without electricity — some for as long as five days — and telephone service was interrupted for 4,000 Southwestern Bell customers.

Jabara Airport sustained severe damage to hangars and 13 airplanes, and minor damage was reported at other area airfields. Dozens of Wichita businesses

'It went that away' is a good phrase to describe what happened to the roof of this hay barn near Pretty Prairie, at far left. The barn owned by Margaret Albright became roofless in the June 19 storm. Photo by Larry Frederick. Left: A large storage shed stands exposed to the elements after the inland hurricane. The opening created by the June 19 wind storm provides a frame for the setting sun on this farm next to K-96, seven miles southeast of Mt. Hope in western Sedgwick County. Photo by Howard Inglish.

reported shattered windows and battered roofs.

In other parts of Sedgwick County, residents of Mount Hope, Valley Center, Park City, Sedgwick and Furley suffered hurricane force winds combined with rain, hail, thunder and lightning.

Grain bins were toppled in Valley Center and Furley. Mobile homes were blown off their foundations, and some were rolled. Wheat trucks slid into ditches, spilling their cargo. Metal outbuildings were hurled across fields, and barn roofs were carried away.

Across Sedgwick County, thousands were affected, and streets completely blocked by uprooted trees and broken limbs were common.

When the storm blazed into western Sedgwick County, it knocked over an Andale grain elevator shortly after 9 p.m.

Five miles north of Andale, Elke Nutterfield was driving on K-96 headed west to visit her in-laws in Hutchinson. She had left Wichita a half hour earlier after visiting her parents. Nutterfield, who grew up in Wichita, lived with her Air Force husband in Alexandria, Louisiana. She was four months pregnant and in Kansas for a one-week visit. It was a visit that took a surprising turn.

"It was still light and I remember driving into one big black cloud when I should have known better," Nutterfield recalled three months later. The rain intensified as she approached Mt. Hope on the western edge of Sedgwick County. "I couldn't see the car several hundred feet in front of me. When the radio said a tornado had been reported near Mt. Hope and to get out of the car, I pulled over.

"I moved over to the passenger side and buckled my seat belt because the car was jumping back and forth. Just as I rolled down the window on the passenger side, the window shattered on the driver's side."

That's when the wind lifted up Nutterfield's 1988 Honda, spun it around and deposited it on the other side of the highway. "After I had my screaming fit, I got out of the car and ran what I thought was a hundred feet, but later I realized I had only gone a few feet."

Because she was pregnant, Nutterfield lay on her back. "I was in a little ravine and was being pelted by the rain. If I raised my head up just a few inches, the wind was really, really strong."

Fifteen minutes later the storm passed, and with a cut on her forehead and black from head to toe with mud, she made her way to other storm victims, who gave her a ride to two Mt. Hope firemen in a fire truck just down the road. "It was really wild," she said of her time in the ravine. "I just remember closing my eyes and holding onto the grass."

Seven miles northeast of Mt. Hope, Charles Basore and his son Richard were harvesting a field south of Bentley when a neighbor warned them of the approaching storm. The two men hurried to their houses to wait out the storm with their families. When they emerged, the farm looked strikingly different.

"It was a straight wind and I've never seen anything like it," Basore said. Sheds were damaged, trees cut down, and the roof and windows of the house were

'I just remember closing my eyes and holding onto the grass.'

— Elke Nutterfield

Wichita Television Weather Forecasters Skip Town Before June 19 Storm

Wichita's top television meteorologists — Jim O'Donnell, Merril Teller and Mike Smith — live and breathe weather, yet they all missed the storm of June 19: KAKE's O'Donnell and KWCH's Teller were at an American Meteorological Society meeting in Colorado, and KSNW's Smith was in Las Vegas at a journalism conference.

"I didn't miss the Wichita wind storm, I just left town," O'Donnell joked. "As I was leaving the airport that morning, a fellow said, 'How come you're not going to stay for the big storms tonight?' He asked if they were going to be strong, and I said, 'yes they are.'"

O'Donnell may have missed the storm, but the storm did not miss his house. He said damage was assessed at about $2,500. "The wind took off the tree, the tree took down the electrical line, and the electrical line tore the box off the side of my house," he said.

Meteorologist John Ridge was on duty at Wichita's KWCH-TV the night of June 19. The day had been hot, with the temperature soaring to 103 degrees.

"It was a situation where you had a low-pressure system moving into the Central Plains, a cold front setting up and the jet stream swooping down from above," Ridge said. "This one was stronger than most. The weather really started gearing up in the west toward late afternoon. The first warning was at 6:13 p.m. for the Goodland area. The last warning we received before the power went out was at 9:23 p.m."

Many people thought there must have been a tornado because of all the damage. "But you have to realize that straight-line winds can do the same thing if they're blowing at 100 miles per hour," Ridge said. "Hurricane-force winds are rated as winds of 75 miles per hour and up. So you could easily call these hurricane-force winds. If you were using a tornado scale, this storm would be classified as F1 damage," as rated on the Fujita scale.

Ridge said a straight-line windstorm tends to hit the Wichita area every three to four years, but none in recent history has had the destructiveness of the June 19 wind shear storm.

'We are airborne.'

— Jim McPheeters

damaged, he said. But the most devastation was evident in the large number of trees that were sheared off at about the 15-foot level. A concrete sidewalk buckled when one large tree was uprooted and landed on the house.

At Bentley Corner, a convenience store, the roof was blown away and several other businesses sustained roof and structural damage. A tree split one mobile home in Bentley in half, and trees and power lines were down, lying across streets and homes. It was a preview of what was to happen minutes later when the storm struck Valley Center, a farming and suburban community of 3,000 located nine miles to the southeast.

The wind-shear storm's intensity was concentrated in the area just north of Wichita and hit hard the communities of Valley Center, Sedgwick, Park City and Furley. It generated winds as high as 114 miles per hour and left several dozen injured, most with cuts and bruises. Valley Center High School sustained more than a half million dollars in damage. Grain elevators, storage bins, barns, a church and mobile homes were twisted and uprooted.

Just before the storm hit, Jim McPheeters and his two youngest children, Colonsay, 11, and Casey, 6, rushed inside their mobile home near the Big Ditch and 85th Street North. McPheeters thought about taking the kids and driving into town to find a shelter. But as the roar of the storm grew, he decided instead to take them to the nearest ditch. As he was on his way out, a window blew out and a couch flew across the living room.

As Casey started out the door, the wind picked him up and threw him into the porch face first. The next thing McPheeters knew, the mobile home was rolling with them in it. "We were airborne," McPheeters said. "I think it probably rolled about one and a half times."

The walls of the mobile home had collapsed on the three, but somehow, none had serious injuries. An exercise bicycle had slammed into Colonsay, injuring her shoulder and collarbone.

Down the road from the McPheeters, Steve and Terri Langwell were trapped inside their mobile home and were pulled out by McPheeters and another neighbor. Terri Langwell was hospitalized for her injuries.

Bill and Beverly Greason's trailer lifted up from its foundation and rolled onto its back. Their granddaughter, Vanessa Ging, recalled the incident succinctly: "I heard Grandma say, 'Hit the ground,' so I did. It all happened pretty quick." The Greasons' daughter, Robin McAllister, who was at Wichita Greyhound Park when the storm hit, said her mother received cuts on her head and spent the night at a Newton hospital. McAllister's daughter, Vanessa, required stitches on her back, while Bill Greason received nerve damage to one leg.

Bill Ackerman and Valerie Peterson — who planned to marry the weekend after the storm — found their mobile home two lots away on top of someone else's car. They decided to abandon mobile home living.

Out on his combine on 109th Street North, Larry

INLAND HURRICANE

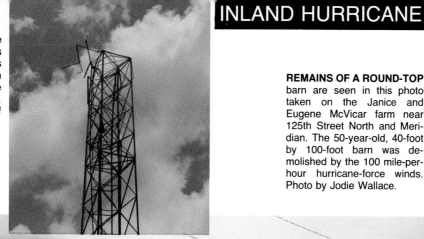

AT HALF MAST, the KFDI tower stands sheared in two on its site near Colwich on the day after the June 19 inland hurricane. Photo courtesy of KG&E.

REMAINS OF A ROUND-TOP barn are seen in this photo taken on the Janice and Eugene McVicar farm near 125th Street North and Meridian. The 50-year-old, 40-foot by 100-foot barn was demolished by the 100 mile-per-hour hurricane-force winds. Photo by Jodie Wallace.

A GRAIN ELEVATOR at the Valley Center branch of the Andale Co-op lies toppled on top of the co-op offices in downtown Valley Center. Photo by Vanessa Mayes.

SITTING ON THE FOUNDATION of her mobile home, Carolynn Comstock ponders what to do next. She continued to live on the site in the summer, first in a tent with a telephone, then in a small camper. Photo by Cynthia Snyder.

WITH ITS ROOF GONE with the wind, this equipment shed north of K-96 near Mt. Hope stands open to the summer sky. The shed was one of hundreds of outbuildings and barns destroyed by the gale-force winds. Photo by Howard Inglish.

INLAND HURRICANE

WORKERS PREPARE to unload insulators flown in by an Ohio company when KG&E depleted its stock a few days after the wind storm. Photo courtesy of KG&E.

GEOMETRIC PATTERNS criss-cross what remains of this hangar at Jabara Airport. Several hangars and 13 airplanes were heavily damaged by the June 19 winds. Photo by David Dinell.

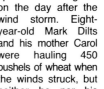

A TRUCK LOAD OF WHEAT awaits clean-up crews in Sedgwick on the day after the wind storm. Eight-year-old Mark Dilts and his mother Carol were hauling 450 bushels of wheat when the winds struck, but neither he nor his mother were hurt. Photo by Mark Dilts.

SALVAGING PERSONAL POSSESSIONS at the Carolynn Comstock home is the order of the day for her daughter-in-law, Mary Cathryn Comstock, on the day after the windstorm. Photo by Donald Comstock.

BROKEN TREE LIMBS nearby block the view of the home of Tim and Karen Travis at 1505 W. 61st N. in north Wichita. Photo by Tim Travis.

THE TIN MAN begins to take form through the craftsman-ship of wood-carver Gino Salerno, who is carving all the major characters from the Wizard of Oz for a display expected to open in the spring of 1991 in Watson Park in Wichita. Photo by Howard Inglish. Storm-sheared trees provided a ready supply of material for Salerno's art. At far left, a Salerno carving of a woman and her dog next to McLean Boulevard catches motorists' attention. Photo by Cynthia Snyder.

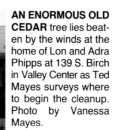

AN ENORMOUS OLD CEDAR tree lies beaten by the winds at the home of Lon and Adra Phipps at 139 S. Birch in Valley Center as Ted Mayes surveys where to begin the cleanup. Photo by Vanessa Mayes.

BROKEN TREES FRAME THE CHURCH of God on the corner of Ash and Second Street in Valley Center on the day after the inland hurricane. Photo by Sheryl Dennett.

A SHEARED UTILITY POLE on Greenwich Road near Furley is a stark reminder of the strength of the winds as the storm blew through eastern Sedgwick County. Most of KG&E's poles along a five-mile stretch had to be replaced. Photo by Joel Klaassen.

KG&E JOURNEYMAN lineman Ray Langlois applies some muscle to the repair task at hand to replace one of the hundreds of poles lost in the storm in Sedgwick County. Photo courtesy of KG&E.

DAMAGE TO THE GORDON EVANS power station near Colwich in northwest Sedgwick County can be seen in this aerial view. The station received major damage to its cooling towers, and was not fully operational until the fall. Photo courtesy of KG&E.

INLAND HURRICANE

A STRING OF VEHICLES LINE this road in northern Sedgwick County as work begins on repairing downed transmission lines. Photo courtesy of KG&E.

AT THE KG&E SERVICE center in downtown Wichita on the night of the inland hurricane, Jim Hopkins, service supervisor, helps coordinate the restoring of power. Keith Clark, underground working foreman, right, and Lee Johnson, service operator, respond to initial outage reports just after the storm moved through Wichita June 19. About 300 helped answer phones at KG&E, and more than 140,000 calls were answered in five days. Photo courtesy of KG&E.

Major Kansas Storms of 1990

FIVE EVENTFUL DAYS marked the Kansas weather of 1990, although a number of smaller storms and tornadoes caused millions of dollars of damage on other days of this busy year that kept meteorologists' heads spinning.

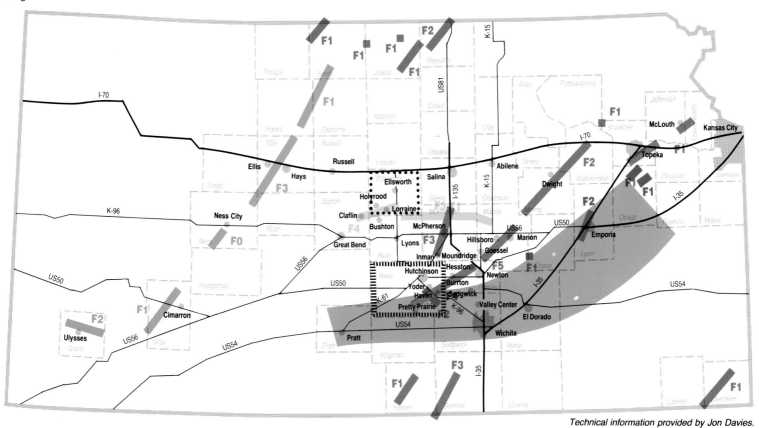

Technical information provided by Jon Davies.

THE TORNADOES OF MARCH 12, 13, and 14, which occurred over a 26-hour period, began the year with a bang as shown on the map in red.

ON APRIL 25, a string of tornadoes along a 180-mile path caused major damage in Ellis County, shown in green.

ON MAY 24, another tornado storm struck central Kansas, shown in yellow, moving in a somewhat unusual easterly direction, and ending within a few miles of the path of the major March 13 tornado.

ON JUNE 7, tornadoes moving in a more traditional northeast direction, shown in dark blue, ripped through several west side neighborhoods and business districts in Emporia, leaving more than 20 injured.

ON JUNE 19, the inland hurricane with winds of more than 110 miles-per-hour, shown in light blue, ripped through half a dozen south central counties, leaving tens of millions of dollars in damage in Wichita and Sedgwick County alone. That same evening, a tornado ripped through Ulysses in southwestern Kansas, moving east-southeast.

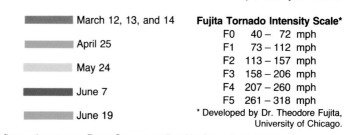

March 12, 13, and 14	
April 25	
May 24	
June 7	
June 19	

Fujita Tornado Intensity Scale*

F0	40 – 72 mph
F1	73 – 112 mph
F2	113 – 157 mph
F3	158 – 206 mph
F4	207 – 260 mph
F5	261 – 318 mph

* Developed by Dr. Theodore Fujita, University of Chicago.

Of these five major storms, Reno County, outlined in the *striped pattern,* was hit by two, the March 13 tornado and the June 19 inland hurricane. The damage paths of these two storms intersected. Reno County, which had a particularly difficult weather year, was hit by three other major storms in April and June.

Floods also hit a number of counties in 1990, but the hardest hit was Ellsworth County, outlined in the *dotted pattern,* where parts of the town of Ellsworth were flooded on July 25.

A RED CROSS worker heads to the agency's truck for more supplies on the farm of Richard and Charlene Janzen west of Hesston. The Red Cross came each day at noon to serve lunch to the volunteer cleanup workers, whose numbers soared to 100 on the days immediately following the March 13 tornado. Donations and food from the Kansas Food Bank helped provide the tons of food for the tens of thousands of meals served over a two-week period. Photo by Richard Janzen.

THE BEATEN HOME of the Schmidt family stands on the day after the tornado in the photo above by Brian Stucky. At right, Diana and Jim Schmidt pose with Ben, 5, and Carrie, 9, in front of their restored home on their farm near Goessel. "I told the kids it would be like camping out" when the family moved into the house eight days after the March 13 tornado, Diana Schmidt recalled. The rebuilding was finished in July.
Photo by Carol Duerksen.

MENNONITE DISASTER SERVICE volunteers pitch in on the construction of a new cattle shed on the Richard Janzen farm, about one mile west of Hesston. The 18-foot by 70-foot shed was rebuilt on the same foundation. Photo by Richard Janzen.

BATTERED AND LEFT UN-INHABITABLE by the March 13 tornado, the former farmhouse of Bill and Leta Royer stands in the background as the Royers and son Bill Jr. pose in front of their new log home southwest of Haven. Photo by Carol Duerksen.

THE TRIP DOWN MEADOW LANE taken by the March 13 tornado smashed beyond repair almost all of the houses and cars on this northeast Hesston residential street. Only five of 15 homes in the neighborhood could be salvaged. Photo by Junia Schmidt. In the photo at the right, a rebuilt Meadow Lane is seen six months after the tornado. Photo by Joel Klaassen.

UNUSUAL HAPPENINGS

THE TOOLS SEEN on the walls and workbench in Floyd Fry's workshop didn't come easy. Cleanup volunteers found five complete sets of the tools scattered over several acres on the Fry farm after weeks of cleaning up debris in the fields. Photo by Carol Duerksen.

BULLS-EYE ACCURACY by the tornado planted this knife from the home of Steve and Vicki Bayless in the limb of a tree several hundred feet away from the Bayless' mobile home northwest of Burrton. Photo by Carol Duerksen.

SAND COMPLETELY FILLED ONE POCKET IN this pair of jeans found on the Eli Bontrager farm north of Burrton after the March 13 tornado. The other pocket was empty. Photo by Merlin Bontrager.

FRUIT JARS WERE LEFT UNTOUCHED in the basement of the Eli Bontrager farm north of Burrton, as seen in photo below. The tornado deposited a trailer next to the jars, sucked up the sub-flooring and demolished the house. Photo by Orvin Bontrager.

THE TORNADO DUG THIS 20-foot trench by pulling a fence post through the yard of a home on the east side of Hesston. Photo by Duane A. Graham.

LIVESTOCK SUFFERED GREATLY in the March 13 tornado. This cow in photo at left was found bruised and with its front feet buried in the ground on the Kevin Neufeldt farm southeast of Inman after the March 13 tornado. Only three yearlings out of 40 cattle survived. This cow was later put to death. "It was the hardest part of the whole storm to see the suffering of the livestock," said Harvey Neufeldt, Kevin's father. "People need to know how sad it was." Photo by Jan Schroeder.

A DAY IN THE LIFE OF KANSAS STORMS

A DAY IN THE LIFE OF KANSAS STORMS is represented in this series of photos. Clockwise from upper left, **A LONE TORNADO SIREN** survived while most trees were battered or broken during the June 19 wind storm when it hit the Mt. Hope Municipal Park in western Sedgwick County. **A TORNADO ROARS** across the countryside southeast of Topeka on June 7, leaving damaged barns and out-buildings in its wake. **A 100-YEAR-OLD BARN** five miles north of Lyons on Highway 14 stands punctured by the tornado that swept through Rice County on March 11. **AS THE RECOVERY AND REBUILDING** begin, volunteers are fed lunch during a cleanup day at the Paul Funk farm east of Inman following the March 13 tornado. Photo credits: Eric Stites, siren; Doug Nelson, tornado; Norma Burfield, barn, and Rosella Funk, volunteer lunch.

Left: Raymond Main views a heavily damaged sports car that was battered when bricks came raining down during the June 19 storm. The car was stored at Valley Center Storage. Photo by Les Anderson.

The garage door is open at the Henri and Mary Trabue residence four-and-a-half miles west of Sedgwick in Harvey County, but not in the way the Trabues would have preferred. The garage received extensive damage when the inland hurricane hit. Photo furnished by Henri and Mary Trabue.

Rowley drove into the blinding rain. "I couldn't see where I was going, so I put my foot on the brake. When I got a big dose of lightning, I could see I was moving backwards."

The combine's platform lifted and the tires slid as the wind blew the combine on the rain-slicked road between Seneca and Meridian. Rowley still couldn't see the end of the 22-foot platform. "A lot of thoughts run through your mind," he said. "Like, how smart am I up on this cab when I should be in a ditch? And how do I get in that ditch?" When he tried to open the door and felt how strong the wind was, he shut it quickly.

Finally, Rowley found a driveway to pull into on North Meridian. Later, Rowley discovered that the combine's mirror had been completely unscrewed by the winds. A friend found the mirror and returned it to him.

Two miles away, Rowley's wife Margie and niece Meredith were in a 1957 Chevrolet, waiting out the storm near 101st and Broadway. Rowley's 80-year-old mother Thelma was next to them in the vehicle she had been driving — a truck filled with wheat. Margie and Meredith had tried to get to the wheat field at 109th and Broadway to drive the truck home, but Thelma Rowley had decided to take matters into her own hands.

The three women waited out the storm north of the intersection of 101st and Broadway. After the storm passed, they found themselves in the middle of the intersection.

Back in Valley Center, Carolyn Wood and her

daughter had tried to find shelter in a nearby basement by crawling across the parking lot at the Valley View Apartments. "Things were flying at us," Wood said. "I saw a big dumpster fly by out of nowhere. I grabbed a hold of a car. I don't know where I would have ended up if it hadn't been for that car — probably somewhere in Butler County."

Near West 53rd Street North and Ridge Road, the storm crashed through a hedgerow south of the home of Gary and Joretta Norris.

"We had just got back in the house when the wind hit," said Joretta Norris, who had taken refuge in the basement with one of the couple's three children. "I was just petrified to come up those steps because I thought the house was gone."

Gary Norris, who had been baling hay about a mile west of the house, had abandoned his tractor and tried for home in a truck, making it to the driveway. Once there, he encountered downed lines and driving rain that made visibility difficult, forcing him to wait out the remaining 15 minutes of the storm in the truck.

When the storm cleared, Norris found his barn demolished and two walls of his concrete, two-car garage broken down. Inside the garage, now resting under the concrete, were a 1981 Pontiac Bonneville, a John Deere riding lawnmower and a deep freeze.

Based on the evidence left behind, Gary Norris is convinced the wind that hit his farmstead was a tornado, not a straight wind. A metal machine shed lost only a skylight, while the barn on the same yard was destroyed. A cedar tree three-and-a-half feet in

'The wind just pushed me off into the ditch. I had no control over the Dodge Ram.'

— Bob Crawford

Jim McPheeters surveys his mobile home that collapsed and rolled with him and his two youngest children inside. The mobile home, located west of the Big Ditch north of 85th Street, was one of dozens in the area damaged or destroyed by the June 19 winds. Photo by Les Anderson.

Approximate path of June 19 inland hurricane.

State Sen. Norma Daniels discusses damage in the Valley Center High School libary with custodians, Harold Eastman, center, and Jerry LaForge. Photo by Les Anderson.

diameter was uprooted, yet a railroad crossing sign in the ground nearby stayed put. The garage collapsed, but the house was not seriously damaged. Compared to the Norris' yard, their neighbor's yard just 100 yards east had very little damage.

With wind speeds of more than 110 miles per hour, the inland hurricane, as it moved through Valley Center, had an intensity approaching that of an F3 tornado.

On June 19, Bobbi Spruill, who operates a day care center south of Valley Center, was not feeling well. "That day, I had severe headaches all day," Spruill said. "I was feeling so bad, and it just got worse and worse. It must have been the barometric pressure. I felt it."

Spruill's inner warning system tested true when the weather alert radio went off, the sirens blared, and the dog started running through all the rooms.

"After my husband saw the dog, he went to the basement," Spruill said.

The Spruills were among thousands who lost their electricity. Theirs stayed off longer than most — four days.

"We used oil lamps, bottled water and ditch water," Spruill said. Even with all the inconvenience, she opened her day care center the day following the storm. "We ate out of the ice chest, sat in the dark and sang songs."

The storm also damaged the Spruills' barn, pasture fence and trees. The family was still cutting up trees in late August.

The spirit of members of Valley Center Assembly of

God was not damaged, although their church was. Within a week of the storm, church members already had put in more than 200 hours cleaning and restoring. Pastor Joseph Voss estimated damage to the church at $40,000.

The roof of the north wing of the church, used for Sunday school and a nursery, was blown onto an empty lot, rendering the facility unusable. The sanctuary also was damaged, as were carpets, floors and ceilings.

"God never said there wouldn't be storms," Voss said in his first sermon after his church was hit, "but He will take us through the storms, and He'll take us through this one."

In Sedgwick — which is located on the Sedgwick-Harvey county line five miles north of Valley Center — eight-year-old Mark Dilts and his mother, Carol, were hauling 450 bushels of wheat in a truck and trailer when the winds struck.

"We had to go real slow; we couldn't really see," said Mark. "I was trying to tell Mom where the lines were, but we went in the ditch because it was all black. The trailer hit a soft spot and tipped over."

Mark said he lay on the floor of the truck with his hands over his head just like he had been taught to do in a tornado.

"All the time we stayed in the truck because the ditch flooded. After the storm, our hired man and the firefighters found us." The Dilts' trailer and hitch received damage, but neither Mark nor his mother was

Left: Dillard Duerksen begins removing pieces from the ceiling damaged from the winds and rain that blasted his Valley Center home. Photo by David Dinell.

Drive-thru parking takes on a new meaning at the parking garage at Wichita's City Hall. One wall of the garage collapsed during the June 19 storm. In October, the City Council decided to tear down the garage and build a new one at a cost of several million dollars after it was determined the existing structure was unsafe. Photo by Howard Inglish.

hurt. "We prayed a lot," he said. Only a small amount of the wheat could be salvaged.

Sedgwick Police Chief Bob Crawford was out on storm watch when a wall of mud hit him — dust, heavy wind and rain.

"I turned around and started to go back into town," he said, "but the wind just pushed me off into the ditch. I had no control over my Dodge Ram. Water was already in the ditch so it just rolled me over. I couldn't get out the door so I just waited till it passed by. The fire truck came out to pick me up, and I pulled my vehicle out later.

Harold Fisher and his wife also ended up in a ditch near Sedgwick. With the winds clocking through the area at 115 miles per hour, they figured the ditch would be a safer place than their car.

Vanessa Mayes of Sedgwick was in the skybox of Wichita's Lawrence-Dumont Stadium when the sirens sounded. "We went below — some to restrooms, some to coolers. Debris started flying at us and we jumped behind a wall. I could feel the grit in my hair. I tried to leave a couple of times, but the sirens went off again."

Once Mayes was able to leave, she had to drive around downed power lines and trees. "Mobile homes were just rolled over along Ridge Road," she said. Flashing lights signaling more downed lines greeted her as she arrived back at her home.

When Mark and Carolyn McGinn came up from the basement of their Sedgwick house where they had taken shelter, they had no idea what awaited them upstairs.

"We could hear the shingles rattle — but we didn't know the roof came off until the water started running into the bedroom," said McGinn. "We were just barely in the basement (when it started) and it just came in one wall, but it lasted a long time."

The McGinns lost one-fourth of their roof, but were able to live in the undamaged part of their house.

The storm got 14-year-old Chad Smiley off the hook. For once, Chad's mother, Tamara Smiley, said, the record albums and clothes littering the floor of his bedroom weren't his fault.

While Chad, his mother, father David Plunkett, and three siblings waited in the basement, the storm strewed part of the roof and pieces of the walls across the lawn and what was once the porch. Chad's room had two large holes, one through an outside wall and one through the attic.

Like many others in the area, the family was without water, electricity and phones. Chief Crawford said the most extensive damage in Sedgwick was to the schools. The band building and most buildings at the grade school were "completely gone."

A few miles to the southeast of Valley Center in Park City, Chisholm Creek Manor, a mobile home park on the northwest corner of town, sustained damage of more than $1 million, and dozens of businesses and homes were damaged.

By 9:30 p.m. the full force of the wind storm was being felt in Wichita, where hundreds of motorists were caught off-guard by the sudden storm. KWCH-TV general manager Sandy DiPasquale, a Kansas resident

Augusta Man Feels Power of Wind Storm

Matt Craft, who lives three and a half miles east of Augusta, was driving home the evening of June 19 when he had a close encounter with powerlines downed by the wind. Approximately two miles west of Augusta, Craft's 1985 Ford pickup took the brunt of the wind-crazed lines.

"I laid down in the seat when they started hitting the roof," Craft remembered. "The roof ended up about two inches above my chest." Craft was able to crawl out the back window of his totalled pickup, and had a broken nose, 120 stitches in his arm, and ligament damage to a finger to show for his encounter with the storm.

Mt. Hope youngsters find a new way to test their bicycling skills as they ride on the roof of what remains of the Greeley Township maintenance building in Mt. Hope. Photo by Eric Stites.

Right: Lynn Decker and his mother Evelyn ponder the damage to his mobile home in Park City's Chisholm Creek Manor, which received $1 million in damage. Photo by David Dinell.

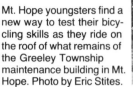

Nancy Shaw's Suburban sits peacefully on South Meridian the day after it struck this utility pole during the June 19 wind-shear storm. The Suburban, with Shaw and a friend inside, took flight during the peak of the storm. Valley Center patrolman Bob Countryman saw the vehicle rise to about 15 to 20 feet in the air when it hit the utility pole. The pole snapped in half. The next day officials found blue paint from the vehicle about 15 feet up the pole. Shaw and the other passenger, a German exchange student, were unhurt after their brief flight. Photo by Les Anderson.

of only one year, was driving with his son when he heard radio reports advising motorists to seek shelter.

DiPasquale pulled into a residential neighborhood and ran from door to door trying to find someone home. As the wind intensified, he decided to take decisive action and, finding a door unlocked, hurried his son down the stairs where they joined a surprised family in the basement. Though surprised, the family welcomed them with true Kansas hospitality, DiPasquale said.

Wichitan Linda Blain was at the checkout counter in the Target store near Towne West when the storm hit. A door opened to the outside and she heard the weather sirens.

"I didn't lose any time," Blain said. "I looked around at all the glass and objects in the store and knew I didn't want to stay there. As I was driving out of the parking lot, the wind hit." But Blain continued on to her home in the Riverside area in central Wichita, four miles away. "I headed east and the car started bouncing back and forth. Big signs were flying across the street like cardboard. Everything seemed to be flying — boxes, branches, papers, all kinds of debris. Some hit my car. The dust just made the sky black. And then the rain came. It was a mess. I made it home and dashed into the house, down into the basement."

At the Wichita Marriott, waitress Christine Ramsey was on duty when the severe winds began their assault on the double-pane glass windows at the front of the hotel.

"The windows came in four inches, went back out, came back in and then just popped and shattered all the way down. It lasted about five minutes," she said.

Emilio Fabico, Marriott resident manager, said about 16 windows were affected. "No glass actually came into the hotel," he said. "The second pane on all the windows held out."

Meanwhile in the Marriott parking lot, the windows of 150 cars didn't hold out. One of the cars belonged to Ramsey. "I had just gotten a brand new car; all my car windows were blown out. There was really no pattern to it either," she said. "It didn't matter if your car window was cracked or shut all the way. Even in the line of cars, it would get some and miss some! It was really weird."

All around Wichita, the lights were going out in neighborhood after neighborhood. The darkness that descended on Kansas' largest city was eerie, but there was little panic.

At Wichita Greyhound Park, about 1,500 patrons had been huddled into the second floor clubhouse area where they were protected by concrete walls. Outside, glass, pieces of roof and rock were flying, damaging some cars in the parking lot. Winning tickets could not be cashed in until three days later when the track reopened.

The winds caused part of the parking garage of Wichita's City Hall to collapse. The City Council decided later in the year to demolish the garage and build a new one.

As Wichitans were groping for candles and flash-

Left: Workmen begin picking up the pieces in what is left of this two-story Southwestern Bell facility in Sedgwick, one of the towns that bore the brunt of the strongest line of winds in the June 19 storm. Photo by John Freeman.

Right: Carolynn Comstock of Furley lived in this tent after her mobile home was demolished by the high winds. She even had her telephone service restored so she could make phone calls while camping out. Later Comstock moved a small mobile home onto the site. Photo by Joel Klaassen.

lights and frantically trying to find a radio or television station on the air, Anne Lassey, principal of Wichita's McLean Science Technology Magnet Elementary School, was at home in Peck in southern Sedgwick County when she got a call about 10 p.m. Lassey was told that half the school's roof was on the lawn. The school was one of several dozen in central Kansas heavily damaged by the wind-shear storm. Lassey was concerned that the computer labs might be in the same wing as the blown-away roof.

When she arrived at the school, she discovered the labs had standing water — some three inches deep, some six inches.

"We worked until about 1 a.m. with nothing but flashlights," Lassey said. Nine parents of students at the school helped out, along with her husband and son. "We just poured the water out and moved the computers to another wing that still had a roof," she said. After servicing, all the computers were saved.

Near the small town of Furley, about 15 miles northeast of Wichita, the wind shear knocked down more than three miles of powerlines along Greenwich Road and pummeled the Furley branch of Andale Farmers Co-op, which suffered severe damage. Replacing the damaged equipment was estimated at several million dollars, according to Allen Mayeske, manager of the co-op.

"The grain elevator is totally lost, the ship machine shed is totally lost and the two liquid fertilizer terminal plants have extensive damage," said Mayeske.

No one was at the co-op when the damage occurred.

Steve Comstock had planned to wait the storm out in his pick-up truck outside his mother's mobile home at the edge of Furley. When a window shattered in on him, he made a dash for the home, crawled in and rolled a couch over himself, according to his mother, Carolynn Kay Comstock. The high winds demolished the mobile home, which was located just east of Greenwich Road, Comstock said, and one wall landed on Steve's bed. Comstock, who was out of town the day her home was destroyed, said she was just thankful her son was okay.

"Some nostalgic things were destroyed — Steve's artwork, pictures, the antique things from Granny and Mom — that hurts. Years of accumulation are just gone. But you can replace material things, not loved ones," she said.

"I functioned because we were cleaning up. Sometimes I'd cry, sometimes I'd be mad; I'd walk and walk and think a lot. You have to have a lot of faith or you wouldn't make it."

After the storm struck Furley, dozens of other towns felt its impact. The storm's intensity began to diminish after it passed through Butler, Harvey and Chase counties. The destruction of a major KG&E transmission line went as far northeast as Matfield Green in southern Chase County as the storm's path paralleled the Kansas Turnpike.

On Wednesday morning, only 10 hours after the first storms hit, the sun was shining in a mostly blue sky. And in the aftermath of one of the worst storms in

One Indirect Death Reported From Wind Storm

The June 19 wind storm resulted in one indirect death, that of Andrew Casten, 24, of Augusta. Casten died of carbon-monoxide poisoning on June 20, the result of fumes coming from a gas generator being used to run a sump pump turned on after the June 19 wind and rain storm. Three family members were hospitalized from the carbon-monoxide poisoning, but recovered fully.

Far Right: A hay barn lies deflated near Sedgwick after the hurricane-force winds lifted it up and set it back down on the Eugene and Janice McVicar farm near Sedgwick. Photo by Janice McVicar.

The Tin Man would have had a field day had he come to Kansas on the day after the inland hurricane. Tin sculptures appeared across a six-county area after the June 19 storm. Photo by John Freeman.

Don Stenli comforts Sylvia Harris after viewing the remnants of their destroyed mobile home at Chisholm Creek Manor in Park City. Photo by David Dinell.

the state's history, neighbors and strangers alike reached out to help one another.

For a while Carolynn Comstock lived in a tent beside the slab of concrete that once was the foundation of her home.

"One morning at 4 a.m. rain hit me in the face and I said there's got to be a better way." She bought a camper in early August, and agencies such as the Mennonite Disaster Services, American Red Cross and the Small Business Administration were helping Comstock resettle; she had no insurance on her mobile home.

Another agency that donated hundreds of hours and thousands of dollars to the relief effort was the Salvation Army. Its mobile unit was on the scene in the north section of Wichita immediately after the first storm hit. Personnel went door to door in Sedgwick, Valley Center, Mt. Hope and Bentley to determine need. Chainsaws and rakes were purchased to help with cleanup; vouchers were supplied for those who lost food, furniture and appliances.

In Sedgwick, Chief Crawford reported that "everybody who had a tractor came out and pushed trees out of the way so we could get up and down the streets to warn of a second storm. And Ray Grindstaff brought in a refrigerated truck to keep things frozen for people."

In Park City, Thad and Robin Everhart opened their grocery store freezers to anyone who needed a place to store their frozen food. "You just help out when needed," Thad Everhart said.

Wichita Public Works officials opened a free site

for tree waste. "This is the only time in the last 25 to 30 years that something like this has been done," said Gail Williams, assistant to the director of public works for the city of Wichita. "And it could be the first time ever."

Relief agencies were on the scene immediately after the storms barreled through — assessing needs and providing shelter, food, clothing, furniture, appliances and help in getting resettled.

In Valley Center, law enforcement personnel from other cities poured in immediately after the winds died down. Those assisting in the patrolling and cleanup efforts that night and the next day came from Hesston, Newton, Derby, Haysville, Wichita and the Wichita State University police departments.

The recovery and rebuilding process took much of the summer.

The McPheeters family of Valley Center replaced their demolished mobile home with a double-wide, and like many other storm survivors, were still replacing furniture and other household goods as 1990 came to an end. They said that after getting over the initial thrill and thankfulness that everyone was okay, it was painful to deal with the loss of valuable possessions. "Being back in our own home is helping us and the children get back to normal as much as possible, but we still deal with it in different ways," Jim McPheeters said.

In Sedgwick, Bill and Beverly Greason, whose mobile home had been smashed without warning, decided to move into Sedgwick into a house. "(The storm put the fear of God into Beverly and our

Pretty Prairie Farmer's Head-On Collision Altered by Winds of Fate

Paul Kemp was driving home from Pretty Prairie with his empty two-ton grain truck the evening of the June 19 wind storm. Kemp, who lives northeast of Pretty Prairie, was within a few miles of his farm house when the storm hit.

"I'd heard there was a storm coming from Pratt, and it had winds of 60-70 miles per hour," he said. "I was headed east, and the winds were coming from the southwest, and blowing so hard I had trouble keeping the truck on the road. All of a sudden I saw headlights coming at me from what I figured was just 20 feet away. I knew we were going to crash head-on, but the next thing I knew the headlights simply disappeared. I realized I didn't have any steering — the wheel felt like it would if the truck was on a lift.

"And that is really what had happened — the truck had been lifted up over the oncoming car. We landed right side up about one-fourth to one-half mile away, in a field. I thought 'This is a strange place to be,' and my directions were all turned around, but I wasn't injured.

"Before too long, the people I had flown over — Fred and Virg Graber — came by to see if I was okay. They confirmed what I was still having trouble believing. They said they had 'bowed their heads and knew it was all over.'

"I know they called the June 19 storm a 'straight wind,' but I feel it was a tornado that lifted my two-ton truck over that car just in the nick of time. I also believe God was watching out for the three of us that evening."

Mobile Home Flips South of Augusta

Pat Schiermeister doesn't remember the sound of the wind hitting her mobile home on June 19. But several months later, her unusual reaction to the sound of an F-16 plane taking off reminded her all too well. "I went into a panic," she recalled. "It must have been the same sound I heard that night. I just don't remember it."

Pat, her 18-year-old daughter Vicki, and Shannon Harelson were in the mobile home four miles west and four and a half south of Augusta when the storm came upon them unexpectedly. "We saw the lightning over Wichita, but we weren't expecting anything here," Pat said. "It sprinkled just a little bit, and Vicki went to her room to close her windows. She was coming down the hallway, looked out the window, and saw the willow tree bent way over. Before she could get to the TV in the living room to turn it on and check the weather, it hit us and flipped the mobile home upside down."

Pat Schiermeister believes it was a tornado, not a straight wind, that invaded their lives that evening. "There was only one other mobile home damaged out here, and it skipped seven others in between ours and theirs," she said. "That, and the sound, makes me think it was a tornado."

Of the three who rode out the mobile home's flip, only Vicki was seriously injured; she suffered a broken collar bone, seven compressed vertebra, and three fractured vertebra in the experience.

Pat and her husband Bruce have replaced the destroyed mobile home with a modular home over a basement. "And I bought a storm alert system," Pat said. "I'm not going to get caught again, not knowing what the weather's doing."

granddaughter, and they didn't want to live in a trailer out there again," Bill said.

While relief and law enforcement agencies helped with the multitude of problems facing humans, there were individuals who were also watching out for the rest of creation.

Wichitan Margie Cartwright and her daughter Corrie had watched during the spring as a pair of orioles built a nest in a tree in their Riverside yard. Four baby birds had hatched the day before the storm.

"Although the limb suspending the nest fell in the wind, the hatchlings survived," Cartwright said. "But one bird fell out two days after the storm and a dog got it, so there were only three left." Margie's husband, Rick, tied up the nest, and the parent birds returned to feed their chicks. Later, the family watched as the young birds grew and learned to fly.

After the June 19 storm, the Kansas National Guard was called in to help in Wichita with the massive cleanup of the tons of debris and tens of thousands of tree limbs that littered streets across the city.

The devastation of so many trees is not a light matter in Kansas where they protect the fertile topsoil from wind erosion. In some areas, the severe damage from the wind storm to wind breaks — so carefully planted more than half a century ago — is virtually identical to damage to wind breaks that received a direct hit from a tornado.

Many trees had to be hauled away, but thousands of others across the six-county area hit hardest by the storm have retained a measure of pride, even in their fallen or sheared state.

Mary and Jim McKenney live on an idyllic seven-and-a-half acres of wooded land north of Park City. Before the storm, they could point to a variety of trees — 64, in fact — including black walnuts, box elder, cottonwood, cedar and mulberry. "The day before the storm, it was like a park — with all the trees and the freshly mowed green grass," Mary McKenney recalled. By the next morning all the trees were down and the place was a mess.

"My reaction was shock," she said. "Just the tree damage, it was so awesome. Everything we had started to do for the summer just stopped. It took us about four weeks to start functioning normally."

Three months after the storm, honey bees have not abandoned their favorite tree on the McKenney farm, even though the tree now lies on its side. In Wichita, tree sculptor Gino Salerno has worked his magic with storm-hit trees along McLean Boulevard, behind the Wichita Art Museum and in Watson Park. The characters for his work in Watson Park couldn't be more appropriate during this wind-tossed year in Kansas: Dorothy and Toto, the Lion, the Tin Man and the rest of the gang — permanent reminders of a storm many Kansans will not soon forget. □

A perilous drive into the Inland Hurricane

By Les Anderson
Editor, *Ark Valley News*

Editor's Note: Ark Valley News *editor Les Anderson wrote this column, which appeared in the June 28 issue of the News, about his attempt to drive into the face of the June 19 inland hurricane.*

As I write this column, it's been exactly one week since The Storm. If anyone had told me a week ago that our area would experience the millions of dollars in damage that it did, I'd have had a difficult time believing them.

Tuesday nights are always late nights at *The News* office. Most summer weeks, we're usually trying to sort through what happened at the city council meeting that night, catch any last-minute details on the swim team's meet or the American Legion baseball team's games. Ironically, the hottest discussion at that night's city council meeting concerned the city's policy on sounding the tornado sirens.

Most of us made it home before the storm hit last week. City officials maintain that the sirens sounded before the electricity went off but none of us in the newspaper office heard anything. We did hear reports of the hurricane-like weather that KFDI's John Wright was describing west of Wichita. He said it was heading our way, so we decided to take cover.

Wife Nancy went home first to make sure our three youngest kids were ready to hit the basement. We invited reporter Kollen Long to take shelter with us but he decided he could make it back to Wichita — a decision he later regretted after enduring the storm with some other unfortunate motorists outside River-lawn Christian Church just north of the bypass on Meridian.

Meanwhile, I waited for oldest son Spike to return from an interview. I unplugged everything electrical in our office and waited impatiently as the sky grew gray, then dirty, then pitch black. Spike and the storm hit the front door of the office with full force at the same time.

Since we had no place to seek protection in the office, we decided to try to make it to our house, about half a mile out of town from Fifth and West streets. That was a mistake. We never made it.

We rocked like a rowboat in his '70 Camaro. We couldn't see anything, except the trees, branches and other debris just as they hit the car. The normal minute-long, five-block drive from Main to Fifth down Ash took about five or 10 minutes but seemed more like an hour.

We drove around fallen trees and huge limbs, then managed to turn west on Fifth. There, it got worse. We were driving into the wind and it seemed as if we weren't able to gain ground. We stopped several times because we couldn't see anything — literally.

We knew there was no way we'd make it home. My mother lives just south of Fifth on Hickory Lane, so we decided to seek shelter there. We knew she'd be in the basement.

The half-block drive down Hickory Lane to her house was no less perilous. It seemed like every tree on the block was in the street. We sat in the driveway for a minute or so, hoping the storm would subside. But it didn't. We watched my mother and stepfather's car rock in the wind, then decided we'd better try to get inside.

Fortunately, she had left the front door unlocked. We barreled down the stairs and collapsed in the southwest corner with them, a neighbor and her two kids.

The storm continued for several more minutes. The pounding against the house and cars seemed to grow louder. Finally, we ventured outside in disbelief at all the damage. After arriving home, we surveyed the damage by flashlight between lightning flashes. The reality of what had happened finally began to sink in.

I can honestly say that I've never been as scared as I was last Tuesday night. Next time, I'll pay more attention to those bad weather warnings. I just hope the people in charge of sounding our sirens do, too. □

> **'Finally we ventured outside in disbelief at all the damage.'**
> — Les Anderson

Blowing in the wind is the answer to where a large part of this structure went following the tornado that struck Ulysses on June 19. This quonset building, a materials storage facility for H&H Construction, is located two-and-a-quarter miles northwest of Ulysses. Photo by Lynette Hickman.

Wind, Hail and Rain Storms:
Late Night Twister Strikes Ulysses June 19

One hour after central Kansas had been battered by the inland hurricane of June 19, another storm began brewing in southwest Kansas.

Without warning a tornado hit Grant County and Ulysses, a community of 5,200 about 75 miles west of Dodge City.

The first notice of the tornado came to the Grant County Law Enforcement Center at 11 p.m. from the Dodge City Weather Bureau. The dispatcher was instructed to sound the sirens and send spotters to the northwest corner of the county.

Perhaps the rapidness with which the storm hit could best be described by Vern Norton, undersheriff for Grant County, who received a call at home a few minutes after 11 p.m. and was advised to go seven miles north to act as a spotter.

Before Norton was even a half-mile from the city limits, the heavy winds forced him to pull over, but he decided to try to make it to the seven-mile mark. Norton said that after he drove three miles, the storm intensified and he decided to take cover at the home of a local farmer, Keith Pucket. Before Norton could reach the house, which was located just off the main highway, the storm hit his vehicle.

"When the storm hit, the Ram Charger was picked up. It didn't move very far; it just moved the vehicle around. Then the rear window of the vehicle broke and I knew I couldn't get out so I tightened my seat belt and decided to wait it out. The vehicle was filled with mud, debris and hail. The inside of the windshield was pitted from all the hail that was moving around inside the vehicle," Norton said.

The Ulysses police had lost contact with Norton shortly after he told them the window had shattered. Norton said this may have been because he could not hear their radio messages over the roar of the storm.

When the winds died down Norton discovered he was only 100 yards away from the shelter he had sought at the Pucket farm house. From the time he had received the call at his residence until he was able to drive back into town was only about 30 minutes.

The storm, which moved east across the northern part of the county, had hit swiftly and had taken the entire community of Ulysses by surprise.

The sirens that warn Ulysses residents had gone off falsely several times in the weeks previous to the storm. In fact, they had gone off at approximately 7:30 p.m. the night that the tornado hit the city. When the alarms sounded again at 11 p.m., some people were in bed and didn't hear the sirens, but most of the citizens took cover, especially once the torrential rains began to fall. The storm hit the city at approximately 11:15 p.m. By 11:20 p.m., many were without electricity and ten minutes later, the debris, torrential rain and power outages were all that was left of the storm.

No injuries were reported, even though the storm left more than $6.5 million in damage to crops, businesses and residential dwellings in its path, according to Lavon Walters, Grant County emergency preparedness coordinator. The area was declared a disaster area by Gov. Mike Hayden, but no outside help for the Na-

'When the storm hit, the Ram Charger was picked up.'

— Vern Norton

F2

Ulysses

Grant

Also blown away in the Ulysses tornado, which struck about 11 p.m. June 19 and was rated F2 on the Fujita scale, was much of the office and shop at H&H Construction. Photo by Lynette Hickman.

tional Guard was needed. The tornado was the first in Ulysses history to hit within the city limits.

Donna Adams was home alone when the sirens sounded. She went to the southwest corner of her basement and covered herself with a sleeping bag. When the wind began blowing, she heard a loud "pop" — a sound she was later to learn was the tornado taking the entire roof off her house.

"I heard the wind whistling through the house, but I thought that windows had been broken. Then the water began to drip into the basement. I was afraid that the pipes had broken," she said.

Adams was too frightened to go upstairs, so she took a flashlight and began to blink it off and on through her basement window. Her only thought was, "I hope someone finds me tonight."

Her neighbor Jeff Trimble came to the window to ask if she was all right. She could only tell him that she wanted to get out of the basement. She heard Jeff break in the front door; when he came to the basement to help her out, he warned her that she would not be prepared for what she would see.

"I had to step over my ceiling when I came up from the basement," she said. "I really wasn't prepared for the devastation in my home."

By 8:00 the next morning, volunteers were already at the Adams' home. Donna is a teacher and many of the staff of USD. 214 showed up to help clear the debris. Members of the Patterson Avenue Church of God were also on hand to help. The storm had taken the roof off the house but not one window had been

> **'I had to step over the ceiling when I came up from the basement.'**
>
> — Donna Adams

broken. Three months after the tornado, Donna and her husband Fred were renting a home and had not decided whether to rebuild their house or start over.

Another family hit by the storm, Verlyn and Dinah Shorter, were watching television in their basement when the sirens sounded. Their children, Duston and Delayna, were asleep upstairs. At first the Shorters believed the sirens were a false alarm, but they decided to be on the safe side and carried the children downstairs. A couple from the house across the street, Karoll and Ann Wagner, joined them in their basement.

While in the basement, they could feel the house shake but did not realize the extent of the damage until Verlyn opened the basement door, looked up, and was startled to find he could see the house next door through the hole in his house.

The Shorters lost their living room, kitchen, dining room and garage in the storm. The neighbors who had taken shelter in their basement were missing only half a dozen shingles off their roof.

For a short time, the Shorters tried to remain in their house while the remodeling was being done. Water damage to the floors from the torrential rains, however, forced them from their home. They rented another residence for several months while the remodeling was completed.

"The storm has made us much more cautious where the weather is concerned. My little boy had nightmares for several weeks after the storm," Dinah Shorter said.

A gaping hole on the south side of the DeKalb-Pfizer Genetics building on the north edge of Ulysses is a solid testimony to the twister's wrath. Photo by Lynette Hickman.

The Red Rock school, which is located approximately 11 miles east of Ulysses, sustained more than $150,000 damage in the tornado. Deciding whether to rebuild was a hotly debated issue at the USD 214 board of education meetings in July, August and September. Although the parents of the Red Rock students and the teachers were in favor of the school being reopened, many citizens and the board were undecided on the issue.

The students who attended Red Rock started school that fall in a vacated school in town. Finally, the board decided in September to rebuild the school.

The tornado destroyed five trailer houses as it swept across the northern edge of the city in an easterly direction. The Dekalb-Pfizer Genetics building received major damage and was left with a gaping hole on the south side of the building. Other businesses with heavy damage were Hickman's, Webbers and Barney Rogers Dirt Contractors.

Farmers in the area were hit extremely hard by the storm. The wheat crop, which had been expected to produce a large harvest, was virtually wiped out in northern parts of the county. The crop loss was estimated at $4 million, but only a small percentage of the farmers did not have crop insurance.

During the storm, Pioneer Electric lost 110 poles, leaving a third of the city without electricity. Pioneer crews worked night and day and power was restored to most of the city by the next evening. By 6 p.m. on Saturday, June 23, all the power had been restored.

Many business and volunteer organizations helped with the cleanup in the city and county. Volunteers from the Mennonite Disaster Service, Red Cross, Russ' Jack and Jill and Pizza Hut were among those who pitched in to help.

Families displaced by the tornado relocated or rebuilt, and most Ulysses businesses completed repairs within a few months, although rebuilding on the Dekalb building continued into the fall.

Just mention the storm on the streets of Ulysses and you will be treated to a variety of stories about how the storm affected each individual. For many years to come, it is likely almost all will be able to tell you exactly where they were and what they were doing at 11:15 p.m. on June 19, 1990. □

'*The storm has made us much more cautious where the weather is concerned.*'

— Dinah Shorter

Near the Reno-Harvey county line, the March 13 tornado heads toward Burrton after hitting dozens of farms in Reno County. Photo by Julie Cargill.

Wind, Hail and Rain Storms:

Five Major Storms Hit Reno County

For Reno County residents, the spring of 1990 was unlike any other. Storm after storm swept the countryside, often undoing heroic efforts to rebuild after previous storms. Farm families who had survived the economic hard times of the Eighties were nearly ready to walk away. By the end of June, some of them had little left to walk away from.

Reno County spawned the devastating March 13 tornado, which ripped northeast to Burrton just over the line in Harvey County, and which continued northeast through Hesston and into Marion and Morris counties before it was done. That storm was followed in Reno County by a hail storm on April 9, a freak wind storm on June 2, another hail storm on June 7, and then the wind shear storm of June 19.

According to Bill Walker, director of Reno County Emergency Preparedness, 1990 was not a typical year. "When you stop and think about it, this is extremely unusual to have these different types of storms. Normally we have a few tornadoes and isolated damage. We've had 25 to 35 million (dollars) in damage this year," Walker said.

The bulk of the Reno County property damage did not come with the March 13 tornadoes, he said, but with the hailstorm of April 9. That storm struck Hutchinson at 5:30 p.m. when a squall line of powerful thunderstorms moved from west to east, generating as many as three tornadoes. Hail larger than golf balls fell on northeast Reno County.

Sandra Heidebrecht and her daughter Angie watched hailstones pile up around the house Sandra

'Hail . . . can just do mindboggling damage.'

— David Chartrand

and her husband John built three years ago on Hutchinson's north edge.

"It was something that you stopped and watched," she said. "It got bigger and louder. You could tell from the size it was going to do some damage."

The double-layer skylights had been designed to withstand large hail, but this hail crashed through one skylight and damaged the outer shell of three others. The hard hail also took its toll on the shake shingle roof.

"It was jagged and came down with so much force; that's why it came through the skylight," Heidebrecht said. Most of the homes in her neighborhood needed new roofs after the storm. "They've had four or five houses going in my addition all summer long. We were feeling pretty sorry for ourselves, but after the Hesston tornado and everything, it's really pretty minor."

While the March 13 tornado covered a large area in several counties, the hail storm — short-lived and confined to north Hutchinson and the surrounding area — did almost as much dollar-and-cents damage. According to David Chartrand of the Insurance Information Institute, the damage to homes, businesses and cars was estimated at $20 million, not including unreported or uninsured losses.

"Hail, if it hits the right part of the city, can just do mindboggling damage," Chartrand said.

The June 2 storm caused far less damage than the April hail in Reno County — estimates were $370,000 — but according to Walker, it was the most bizarre storm he has seen.

"I've never seen another one like it. It was almost

like everything was happening in slow motion," he said. "It could have been a disaster, but there was no loss of life. You can see a tornado or a thunderstorm coming. There's no way you can warn about this."

From 9 a.m. to noon that Saturday, winds up to 100 and 110 miles per hour were clocked in Hutchinson and northeast Reno County. Windy conditions had been forecast, but the clear, blue skies gave no warning of the disaster to come, the result of a strong pressure gradient between storms in Texas and the Dakotas.

Three hours of sustained violent winds caused damage throughout Reno County, with heaviest damage reported in an area bordered by Abbyville, Nickerson, Buhler and Haven. In Buhler trees damaged three houses, and an auction barn lost part of its roof.

Hutchinson got the worst of it. Roofs of houses and businesses were damaged. Traffic lights across Hutchinson and South Hutchinson were disabled. Livestock watering tanks were blown blocks away from a farm supply store in east Hutchinson. In downtown Hutchinson, windows were blown out of stores and a light pole was whipped from its mounting next to the Wiley Building.

In northwest Hutchinson, Will and Nancy Wilson came home to find their tall maple tree on top of their house. Limbs stabbed the roof, breaking rafters; uplifted roots buckled the driveway. The tree trunk was heavier than the truck used to move it, and it would be more than two months before roof contractors, busy with other storm repairs, could find time to repair the roof.

Roofs were damaged at the Kansas State Fairgrounds, businesses on 30th Street and at the south end of Main Street were hit, and areas with many trees, such as Hyde Park in north central Hutchinson, suffered heavy damage. Carey Park, in the south part of the city, also sustained heavy tree damage.

"It was trashed," said Hutchinson Police patrolman Gordon Smith, adding that he and other officers — including some who were off duty — had all they could handle in a chaotic situation.

The storm marked the first time the Reno County Emergency Operations Center was put into action. Twenty city and county officials received calls and coordinated action at the center. National guardsmen, already conducting exercises, were enlisted to help restore order.

Emergency officials recorded more than 100 power outages, mostly at homes, seven broken gas lines, scores of downed and damaged trees and power poles, and numerous damaged traffic signals and railroad crossing arms. The powerline problems continued as lines remained entangled. Kansas Power and Light officials said as many as 10,000 customers were without electricity for part of the day. Crews from four Kansas cities helped restore power.

Even after a tornado, a hail storm and a freak wind storm, the violent weather wasn't through with Reno County. On June 7, less than a week after the wind storm ripped through Hutchinson, part of a storm that would later hit Emporia with tornadoes grazed

Far Left: Trees nestled against the parsonage of the Pleasant Grove United Methodist Church north of Haven offer clear evidence of the power of winds that roared through Reno County on June 2. The house was repaired — for the second time in less than three months. On March 13, the roof was damaged when the tornado that would later strike Hesston roared across the edge of a nearby field. Photo by Boneva Hammar.

Above: An outbuilding lies crumpled and sandwiched between trees on the Don Fischer farm near Pretty Prairie after succumbing to the ferocity of 115-mile-per-hour winds of the June 19 inland hurricane. For Fischer, it was his second major encounter in 1990 with Kansas winds: The March 13 tornado first touched down within several miles of his farm, and he took the cover photo for this book. Photo by Don Fischer.

In Hutchinson, the sidewalk on Main Street is littered with debris from roofs of nearby businesses on the day after Reno County was hit by the June 2 wind storm, one of five major storms to strike the county in 1990. Photo by Monty Davis, Hutchinson News.

southeast Reno County. Hail flattened hundreds of acres of crops, some of which belonged to Galen and Donna Schrag, who live northeast of Pretty Prairie.

Schrag said the storm "backed in from the east, where you don't expect it. It hailed for 55 minutes. There was no wheat standing."

Meteorologist Jon Davies confirmed that a tornado with 100 mile-per-hour winds hit near Pretty Prairie that night and moved southeast to northwest, a condition he termed "very unusual."

The Schrags, still recovering from a 1985 bankruptcy, lost more than 200 acres of wheat in the June 7 hail storm, making it the most financially devastating storm for the Schrags.

Just as the Schrag family was beginning to recover from the June 7 storm, June 19 found Pretty Prairie in the path of the wide storm that wreaked havoc in Wichita and Sedgwick County.

Donna Schrag was in the house, and Galen Schrag had just returned when the storm hit. She ran to the basement and he held the back door shut, fearing that the wind would tear the back porch from the house. When the Schrags emerged, they saw that the wind had damaged shed and barn roofs, stripped trees and knocked the power out.

That same evening Michael and Lisa Childs of Nickerson were driving home from Wichita with Larry Balsmeier, Michael Childs' uncle, when heavy rain forced them to stop. Radio reports indicated a storm near Kingman. When they heard of a tornado sighting near Mount Hope, they decided to abandon the car.

"I grabbed my son out of the car seat, and the wind kind of picked us both up and just threw us in the ditch," Lisa Childs said. "I put one foot out to run, and the wind blew me into the ditch."

Michael Childs began running to a large truck that had stopped behind them, hoping to call for help. He stopped just before the truck was blown over. They didn't see the truck again.

A metal object, possibly a road sign, struck Balsmeier's leg, severely wounding him. He was treated and released two days later from Hutchinson Hospital.

In Reno County most of the night's damage was caused by wind, not tornadoes, and weather observations from the west and south spelled trouble for Sedgwick County. Winds of 116 miles per hour were reported near Kingman, 90 mile-per-hour winds were reported near Turon, and Pratt reported 65 mile-per-hour winds.

Wynn and Linda Bailey, owners of Cheney Marina on the southeast corner of Cheney Lake, saw lightning to the west and abruptly ended their ski outing. Minutes out of the water, Bailey checked the marina television for a storm report. Radar clearly showed the storm bearing down on the other side of the lake.

Linda Bailey had gone to their nearby house and came back to pick up her husband in a car. He got in and the storm hit.

"If we would have opened the door, I think we would have lost it," she said. "There was so much

'I put one foot out to run, and the wind blew me into the ditch.'

— Lisa Childs

102

Above: An uprooted tree rests on the roof of the home of William and Nancy Wilson in west Hutchinson following the June 2 wind storm. Photo by William Wilson.

Far Left: Merchandise in Grandma's Picket Fence in Wiley Plaza in Hutchinson lies scattered after the store's windows were blown out by the high winds of Saturday morning, June 2. Photo by Monty Davis.

storm going on you couldn't see what was going on around you."

The Baileys rode out the storm with their children, a hamster, a cat and a dog. The wind let up, and Wynn Bailey checked the marina wind meter. It was "blitzed" at 125 miles per hour, Linda Bailey said. He reset the meter, and it later registered winds of 107 miles per hour.

The lull between storm blasts was eerie, Linda Bailey said.

"I was raised on the East Coast. It was almost like the eye of a hurricane," she said.

The former owner of the marina, P.J. Haynes of Wichita, was driving to the lake when his small truck was swept from the road. He drove on after the storm passed, and helped assess the damage.

The boats and docks of the marina were shoved together "like a jigsaw puzzle," Linda Bailey said.

On the morning of June 20, more than 60 boat owners helped clean up the mess.

"The next night every boat was accessible. Within 24 hours, we had things looking normal," Linda Bailey said. It took 10 days to get the dock operating again.

The Baileys, who operate in conjunction with the state, were awaiting insurance settlements in August. The storm caused an estimated $150,000 damage to the marina property, she said.

Across the lake, the Ninnescah Yacht Club and its members sustained thousands of dollars in damage to boats that were piled on the shore.

Cheney State Park officials reported five overturned trailers, one with a woman trapped inside for a short time.

For the Schrags, the June 19 storm was almost the final blow. They considered taking the insurance payments and walking away from the farm. Schrag spent a sleepless night, walking the shredded farmstead where he was born and raised.

"He said, 'Go ahead and sleep if you can, and be ready to pack some bags in the morning,' " Donna Schrag said.

Then Mennonite Disaster Service volunteers arrived, Schrag said. They helped rebuild, gave financial help, and most important, gave him moral and emotional support. Many were local Mennonites the Schrags knew. They decided to stay and keep working the 50-cow herd.

"How do you walk away from that?" Schrag said.

He cited a passage of the Bible: "It is better to give than to receive."

"But when you sit here and have to receive, you wish you were the one who could be giving."

Still, the weather was not done with the Schrags. They had the farm nearly back to normal by August 7, then at about 5:15 p.m. on August 10, Schrag was milking when the barn roof began "bouncing." Another "minor" storm blew out of the east.

"Finally it quit. I go outside and another half of the barn is gone," he said.

This time, Schrag saw that a section of a lean-to was about to blow off. He drove a tractor up to it and set a front-end loader bucket on top of it. The roof

Walk-in traffic combined with this style of window shopping is probably not what officials at Reffner's in downtown Hutchinson had in mind for Saturday shopping on June 2. Repairmen Jim Bolyard, right, and Tirso Galindo, of Whitewing Construction Co. check out the damage. Photo by Monty Davis.

didn't blow away.

The storm completed the damage started June 7 on the roof of a "loafing shed" where cows escape the elements. The June 7 hail damaged the north half. It was repaired, but the August 10 storm blew off the south half.

By August 18, the Mennonite Disaster Service had come to help again, and in one morning, with scrap materials, the shed was repaired.

The Schrags said they recorded the names of those who helped, and sent thank you cards, but knew they could never properly thank them all.

"I hope no one was left out," Mrs. Schrag said.

'I hope no one was left out.'

— Donna Schrag

By August, estimated damage from the June 19 storm in Reno County was $640,000 with the total figure expected to climb. The County Emergency Operations Center recorded losses for official disaster relief needs. The county commission declared a state of emergency for all three major storms. Reno County was included in a state disaster area for the March 13 and June 19 storms.

Walker of emergency preparedness said the March 13 tornado damage was the easiest to assess. It struck a narrow path through the county, while the June 2 and 19 storms were widespread.

Walker said that it was a "godsend" that there were no storm-related deaths in Reno County. Part of the miracle is due to an increased respect for storms in south central Kansas, part of "tornado alley." □

Far Left: A mail carrier might consider a boat to reach patrons on this Ellsworth route following the July 26 flood. Photo by Bonnie Kralik.

Left: "You clean and you clean and you clean, and you can still clean, and you just never get it all," Bonnie Kralik said of the water damage to their mobile home in southwest Ellsworth. Bonnie and Troy Kralik were able to put their furniture above water level, but the damage to carpet and insulation was extensive. Photo by Bonnie Kralik.

Wind, Hail and Rain Storms:
Sudden Flooding Surges Through Ellsworth in July

As of late July Mother Nature had not finished her attacks on the people of central Kansas. Heavy rains that began late on July 25 in Lincoln and Ellsworth counties by morning had pushed the Saline and Smoky Hill rivers out of their banks, flooding 10,000 acres.

The National Weather Service reported 10 inches of rainfall that night in southern Lincoln County, and the small town of Tescott 15 miles northwest of Salina suffered flood waters up to three feet high from the swollen Saline River. The town was also attacked the next day by three more inches of rain and marble-sized hail. That storm caused the river to crest four-and-a-half feet above flood stage. The flooding affected about a dozen homes and businesses and caused power and natural gas outages.

The seven inches that fell in Ellsworth County the night of July 25 was enough to create the worst flood in half a century and force nearly two dozen families from their homes in Ellsworth, 35 miles west of Salina. By late afternoon on July 26, the Smoky Hill River was six feet above flood level.

While many residents reported hearing water raging through the night, it was not until daybreak that most saw the rapidly rising waters, which would crest only a foot lower than the flood of 1938. Road closings began about 9 a.m. and a newly constructed bridge on K-14 had to be closed much of the day. Many residents continued to work in waist-deep water to save what they could from their homes. Those who refused to leave their homes received provisions from small-boat patrols.

Water continued to rise during the afternoon and crested about 3 p.m. at 26.06 feet, a foot higher than the 1951 flood. Floods are not unknown in this part of Kansas and a sign marking the original townsite of Ellsworth — which was destroyed by a flood in 1866 — was surrounded by water in the 1990 flood. The water began receding about 4 p.m. on July 26 and was back within its banks by the next morning.

The Northern Kansas Chapter of the American Red Cross reported that two people were injured in the floods and that one home was totally destroyed. Homes and mobile homes with either major or minor damage were tallied at 26. The Red Cross shelter for those evacuated helped 32 people and served 369 meals.

Cleo Rathbun of Ellsworth was one of those aware of the heavy rainfall in the early hours of July 26. He got up at 3 a.m. to move gardening equipment out of a shed in his yard, but it was already under water. Neighbors and friends helped him load furniture on a truck and trailer and transport it to the National Guard armory, which by that afternoon would be isolated by water. They were able to save all the furniture from their own home, but not from a rental property next door.

Eleanor Rathbun had lived at this location since 1935. Although there had been water in her basement and surrounding the house at times (particularly in the big flood year of 1951), she had not experienced water in the ground floor of her home since 1938.

Far Right: Flood waters nearly top the fence north of the National Guard Armory in Ellsworth. Photo by Bonnie Kralik.

Right: An unwelcome, temporary lake covers the yard of George Soucek in southwest Ellsworth. Photo by Bonnie Kralik.

'You can walk around outside and it smells like dead fish.'

— Bonnie Kralik

Since no warning was issued by the emergency preparedness office, some residents, like Karen Shriner and her son Kevin, had no hint of trouble until they awoke Thursday morning. Shriner estimated the water was less than three inches deep on the main floor, ruining carpets but not furniture. Shriner's basement, however, was furnished, and most of her possessions there were ruined. Oddly, the dishes in two china cabinets were unbroken, even though the cabinets were floating.

I.D. Creech, Ellsworth's city administrator, believes many residents were reluctant to believe their homes were threatened. After all, many had never seen it happen before.

When Bonnie Kralik left for work at 6 a.m., she did not realize the river would be a threat. Her husband Troy called her at work about 8 a.m. to say the water was rising. At 11 a.m. he called again, asking her to come home because the water was about to come into their mobile home. Although they did not have time to move furniture out, they put it above water level. Their main loss was the carpet and insulation.

"You clean and you clean and you clean, and you can still clean, and you just never get it all," Bonnie said. "The kitchen floor, I scrubbed it three times with a mop and three times on my hands and knees, and probably the next week I cleaned it twice more and I still had filthy water. You can walk around outside and it smells like dead fish."

Small sheds, lawn mowers and a camper were shifted considerable distances by the waters. George Soucek owned some geese and pygmy goats, which had to be moved to higher ground.

Many volunteers, including officers and inmates from the Ellsworth Correctional Facility, hauled sandbags to areas which still could be saved, evacuated residents and helped move out furniture.

"You've got to learn from everything," Creech said. "It appears that emergency communications for the county need to be reviewed. There were some wrong assumptions made by the residents, the county and the city."

A zoning regulation passed in 1989 for houses in the floodplain will ensure that future buildings will be safer than present ones. A possible preventive measure would be the building of a channel around the city, but Creech says the cost would be "millions of dollars."

Some residents favor building a dike. "In most cases it would probably be most effective," Creech said. "In this case I don't know whether it would have."

□

A Hesston football spirit banner shouts encouragement to all who will take it to heart, even the relief workers headquartered in the school following the tornado. Here Salvation Army workers take a break from efforts to help survivors. Photo by Larry Swank.

Red Cross

Round the clock help
Emergency assistance to disaster
    victims
Does the job

Claims work service for veterans
Remembered world wide
Open to the public
Saves lives
Supports people

Micah Rose
Danny Schroeder

Relief and Recovery:
Agencies, Businesses Rise to Storms' Challenge

Many people lost food, shelter, clothing and electricity in the storms that hit Kansas in the spring and summer of 1990. But those whose jobs were helping restore those necessities as quickly as possible found themselves without another basic need — sleep.

"You don't get much sleep the first few days. It really keeps you hopping," said J. Sharon Powell Quincy, assistant director of emergency social services for the Midway-Kansas Chapter of the American Red Cross.

The chapter, which serves Harvey, Sedgwick, Kingman, Harper and Sumner counties, sent a van of supplies to Hesston the same night the tornado struck and began calling damage assessment employees to report the next morning. More than 200 volunteers and staff members helped serve thousands of meals and provide other services in the days following the storm. The Red Cross also provided services to victims of the June 19 windstorm.

"We haven't had anything like this in the 17 years I've been here," Powell Quincy said. "Now we have two (disasters) in a row."

Employees of Kansas Gas and Electric Co., based in Wichita, also faced unprecedented challenges. The June windstorm initially knocked out power to some 60,000 customers in Harvey, Sedgwick and Butler counties. The company rated the storm as the worst in its 80-year history.

Crew members who had worked all day that Tuesday went back out after the storm hit and worked all night and all the next day. Hundreds more massed together to answer phones, order supplies and provide support services to the crews and their counterparts called in from neighboring utilities and towns.

"They were working on about five, six hours of sleep the whole week," said KG&E regional manager Don Elliott. "We all lived on about five hours sleep for several days."

Red Cross and KG&E personnel were among the thousands representing social service agencies, government offices, businesses, utility crews and insurance adjusters who were on the scene within minutes and hours after storms struck.

The massive amount of damage kept those people working around the clock and calculators ticking trying to add up Mother Nature's price tag. Although the heaviest workload was in the days immediately following the storms, the disasters piled up enough work to keep some busy for months. KG&E did not expect to have a major transmission line between Wichita and Matfield Green back in operation until early 1991.

Accurate damage figures were hard to come by for a variety of reasons: only preliminary estimates were turned in to the Kansas Division of Emergency Preparedness; numbers varied from agency to agency or were not available; agricultural losses could not be finalized until after fall harvest; and some businesses and organizations were still processing paperwork and making repairs months afterwards. It was estimated that more than $150 million worth of damage was wreaked by tornadoes, wind, hail and floods in about four months.

This poem by Micah Rose and Danny Schroeder is part of a book written and compiled by the 7th grade class of Mrs. Shannon Zuercher in Hesston. In the forward, Mrs. Zuercher wrote: "This book grew out of our experiences with the tornado. The tornado affected many of our students, from minor losses to the devastation of homes. Writing is a way of processing some of the students' feelings about this incident which has happened to Hesston. March 13, 1990 will always be etched in the minds of our students."

107

A Star Lumber & Supply truck returns for another load of debris, while a farm truck receives its burden of tornadic trash. Hundreds of businesses and farmers with heavy equipment showed up following the storms to assist in cleanup procedures. Photo by Vada Snider.

Town people provided shelter, comfort, and food.
Out of town people provided the same.
Red Cross came with helpful supplies.
National Guard guarded the town and patroled the streets.
Army-Salvation provided some clothes.
Disaster Service (MDS) helped with the actual clean-up.
Out of town schools raised money.

By
Andrea Weaver
and
Rusty Whitcher

Andrea Weaver and Rusty Whitcher explain what tornado recovery meant to them in this contribution to the 7th grade book.

Following the March 13 tornadoes, Gov. Mike Hayden declared 11 counties disaster areas: Geary, Harvey, Jefferson, Jewell, Marion, McPherson, Morris, Reno, Saline, Shawnee and Sumner.

The state disaster declarations enabled counties to use state resources, such as the Kansas National Guard, and were the first step in applying for federal assistance through low-interest loans. The National Guard provided much assistance following the Kansas storms.

In Hesston from March 13 to 15, the hours worked in security and traffic control by the National Guard were the equivalent of 137 days. One "man day" costs about $120, according to the National Guard office in Topeka.

Following the Emporia tornado, the National Guard spent another 100 man days for security and traffic control. It provided a generator after the June 19 windstorm for a nursing home in Sedgwick County.

Because of the large amount of tree debris the June storm caused in Wichita, National Guard troops were sent there in July to help city crews. The Guard racked up 242 man days in Wichita, the tab of which was picked up by the federal government because those guardsmen were on annual training status at the time.

The cleanup in Wichita required about 30,000 labor hours by as many as 150 guardsmen and about 300 city employees reassigned for the task, according to the city of Wichita public works department. The cleanup, which began June 20, lasted until Aug. 5 when brush dumping at the landfill was shut down. An estimated 13,500 loads of brush were hauled to the

landfill, about 9,000 of those by government personnel and the rest by private citizens, the city said.

Also keeping tabs on assistance rendered were the Red Cross and Salvation Army.

By noon the day after the Hesston tornado, the Salvation Army had arrived with two truckloads of materials — food, clothing and bedding. Two additional truckloads were delivered in the next two days. About 3,000 meals were served in the first three days — some 3,000 cups of coffee, 2,500 sandwiches and 840 doughnuts, according to the Salvation Army's Wichita office.

Salvation Army units from Wichita, Salina, El Dorado, Newton, Kansas City and Hutchinson went to Hesston. Eighteen volunteers worked 377 hours.

After the June windstorm, units from Wichita, Hutchinson and Coffeyville assisted about 3,400 people and went door to door in Sedgwick, Mount Hope, Valley Center and Bentley to determine need, an official said. Twenty-three volunteers put in 475 hours.

Hundreds of families lost food because of electrical outages and the Salvation Army spent about $14,000 buying 21 meals each for 361 families (1,438 individuals). It also purchased chain saws to help clean up tree debris. For the first time that officials in Wichita can remember, the Salvation Army made a public plea for donations to help cover the costs.

Donations poured in after the Hesston tornado. But eight weeks after the windstorm, only a little more than $5,000 had been donated specifically to the Salvation

The awesome, painstaking task facing volunteers who came to help clean up the tornado's ravages is depicted in the photos on this page by Vada Snider.

Army for that disaster. Money from general donations likely would be transferred to cover the disaster expenses, the official said.

The American Red Cross reported serving almost 14,000 meals after the Hesston tornado and 335 after the June windstorm. About 225 volunteers and staff members worked 4,500 hours in Hesston and 40 people spent 510 hours in service in June.

The Red Cross also provided vouchers to disaster victims for purchase of clothing, food, furniture and other necessities. Although there are no income guidelines for the vouchers, they generally are given to low-income and uninsured people, said the Red Cross' Powell Quincy. The agency had 112 families register for assistance in Hesston and 42 families after the June storm, she said.

Estimated relief costs were $108,000 for the Hesston tornado and $35,550 for the windstorm. Like the Salvation Army, the Red Cross reported receiving many donations for the tornado, but much less — about $1,000 — in donations for the windstorm. The Red Cross' national organization will pay for the costs exceeding donations, Powell Quincy said.

Likewise, the Northern Kansas Red Cross chapter is to be reimbursed by the national organization for about $28,000 of the nearly $30,500 it spent to assist victims of the Emporia tornado and floods in Ellsworth and Tescott.

The Hesston Tornado Fund set up by the Hesston Ministerial Alliance received $332,466 in donations from individuals, businesses and groups, including schools and churches.

The Red Cross served 764 meals in Emporia and 369 to flood victims. Ninety-two volunteers and staff served more than 1,000 hours after the tornado and 29 Red Cross personnel worked 676 hours in Ellsworth and Tescott. About 15 families applied for assistance from each of the two disasters.

In addition to social service agencies, businesses also lent helping hands and resources after the storms. Dozens of restaurants donated food. After the Hesston tornado, Cherry Orchard furniture of Wichita donated 5,000 square feet of warehouse space and the manpower and vehicles to pick up and store donated furniture.

"We wanted to help," said owner Marino Garci. "We had the trucks and the room. Sometimes you can be the missing link."

Employees spent about two weeks picking up furniture and it took three months for it to filter out of the warehouse as homeowners slowly rebuilt, Garci said. Old mattresses and other donations left untouched were given to AmVets. Cherry Orchard didn't keep track of its expense during the ordeal.

"We don't put dollar figures to things like that," Garci said.

Dillons Stores, Inc., based in Hutchinson, also provided assistance to storm victims.

A semi-trailer load of bottled water was hauled from a Hutchinson warehouse to Hesston hours after the tornado struck.

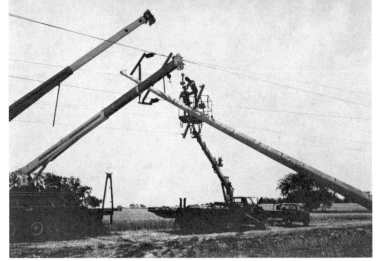

Symmetry of destruction and recovery: Downed power lines northeast of the Gordon Evans power station, left, and replacement of lines and poles by crews for KG&E, give an idea of the massive task facing the Wichita-based utility following the June 19 wind storm. Photo of downed lines by Kenneth Kroupa. Photo of repair work courtesy of KG&E.

Poles are meant to hold up lines, but when the wind broke this pole near Valley Center in half, the lines returned the favor. Photo by Shawn Spruill.

"We've done this sort of thing in past emergencies in the area. We felt compelled to do it and we did it. We helped some people who needed it," said Ken Keefer, spokesman for Dillons.

John Baldwin, president of the division, "literally led the convoy," Keefer said. Baldwin and a co-worker spent several hours navigating blocked roads that night in order to deliver the semi and its 4,000 gallons of bottled water to Hesston. In the June 19 windstorm, Dillons donated 1,000 gallons.

The Dillons store in Newton allowed Salvation Army workers to take the food they needed to feed victims and relief workers in the days following the tornado.

Keefer said the chance to help was gratifying.

"We owe this state and an awful lot of people. When we can give something back, we jump at the chance," he said.

Days after the tornado, Dillons began taking donations from customers across the state, which the company matched with $10,000. The combined total of more than $20,000 was then given to the Hesston Disaster Relief team, which distributed the funds through the American Red Cross, the Salvation Army and the Hesston Tornado Victims Fund throughout the seven counties affected by the storm, Keefer said.

But Mother Nature doesn't play favorites, and with the June windstorm, Dillons found itself also a victim. Three stores received damage, and the store at Douglas and Meridian in Wichita went without electricity for more than two days and was closed to customers for

three. About $40,000 worth of perishable food was donated to the Kansas Food Bank.

"That was a nightmare," said manager Tom Seymore. "We had to restock everything. When you lose refrigeration like that, water comes from everywhere. There was a lot of mopping in the dark with flashlights and Coleman lanterns."

The whole ordeal was worse than when Seymore lived for two days and nights in a Dillons store in the early '70s during a bad snow storm. "One of those in a lifetime is enough," he said of the 1990 incident.

Although Dillons' problems paled in comparison to KG&E's, utility officials likely were expressing similar sentiments. The electric company was hit with a double whammy in 1990.

The Hesston tornado knocked power out for more than 3,000 KG&E customers. More than 230 power poles were down on major transmission and distribution lines, and major power lines near Burrton, Goessel and Hesston were torn out. In one 19-square-mile area, all power lines were down.

Crews from throughout KG&E's system, from KPL in Hutchinson, Topeka and Emporia and contract linemen from Wichita and Tulsa were called in.

Less than an hour after the tornado struck, linemen had completed first repairs to transmission lines serving the Hesston substation. In three days, all power was restored. The tornado caused $4.5 million damage to KG&E, an official said.

But the tornado proved to be only a practice run for the June windstorm when Mother Nature leveled a

Part of the recovery process for almost all storm survivors is finding valued possesions that represent pieces of their lives. In this search through some of the rubble left by the tornado in Hesston, Lynn Jackson and Brenda Nebel marvel at the discovery of an unscathed box of microwave popcorn in Nebel's otherwise destroyed kitchen. Photo by Vada Snider.

The National Guard controls access to Hesston streets so that residents will not lose more than the storm had already taken from them. Photo by Duane Graham.

devastating blow to the 80-year-old company.

When the temperature rose to 103 degrees on June 19, the summer's high at that point, KG&E customers pushed the system load to its highest of the year. Three crews were held over from the afternoon to restore service because transformers had blown and switches had tripped.

All customers had lights by 8:30 p.m., about the time weather reports of 115-mile-an-hour winds at Kingman were aired. Roger Holt, Wichita line duty supervisor, told crews to stay on duty a while longer. Within minutes after the windstorm hit, 10 pages of computer printouts piled up with the hundreds of lines showing circuit lockouts and substation alarms.

Probably more than 60,000 customers lost service as winds roared over 1,260 square miles of KG&E service territory in about 30 minutes, causing some $20 million in damage.

The company's Wichita, Newton and El Dorado divisions were the hardest hit from the June 19 wind shear storm. About 1,000 major transmission poles and another 200 distribution poles were down.

The Gordon Evans power station near Colwich received major damage to both its cooling towers. The Unit 1 tower was back in full operation July 13, but repairs to Unit 2 were not completed until three months after the storm.

Nearly five miles of a major transmission line that connects to a line that goes to Oklahoma was down and took more than three months to repair. But the heaviest damage was to 40 miles of a 50-mile major

transmission line between Wichita and Matfield Green that connects to Kansas City. Traffic along that line was rerouted and restoration was not expected to be completed until early 1991. It took more than a year to build the line originally, and because of the storm damage it essentially had to be rebuilt, a KG&E spokesman said.

Although there was long-term damage, KG&E's first priority was restoring electrical power to its customers. A work force that grew to 1,300 helped restore power to most customers within four days after the storm. In all, 62 crews from across Kansas and Oklahoma replaced 300 miles of electrical lines.

By Saturday morning following the Tuesday night storm, only about 3,000 of the initial 60,000 without power were still without it. The final hookups were made by the end of the month. About 10,000 customers had power in less than 12 hours after the storm. One of those was Ferroloy Foundry Inc., which expressed its appreciation in a letter to KG&E:

"We were without power about 1 1/2 hours. Don't know if you guys are good or lucky, but we had a furnace full that could have turned into a 12,000 pound paperweight. Thanks!"

About 300 helped answer phones at KG&E and provided support to line crews. In five days, more than 140,000 phone calls were answered, not including customer calls transcribed from recorders.

Some customers called in calmly just to let someone know they were still in the dark. One woman

'There was a lot of mopping in the dark with flashlights and Coleman lanterns.'

— Tom Seymore
Dillons

Seventh graders Mel Wright and Jenny Wieland express their feelings about Dillons Stores in this illustrated 'Fact or Fiction' piece for their class project following the tornado in Hesston.

called to say she and her teenage son hadn't talked so much in a long time, KG&E said.

KG&E's purchasing department had the job of arranging for more than 400 hotel rooms for crew members called in from other areas and getting them supplies, which vendors put people on overtime to get. An Ohio company sent a plane load of insulators hot off the assembly line. Poles were trucked in from Missouri and Kansas and Oklahoma utilities. Another function of purchasing was to sell storm damaged materials for salvage — it collected almost 2 million pounds of aluminum wreckage from the storm.

Other KG&E employees kept busy taking food, beverages and things such as Chapstick and suntan lotion to line workers so they could keep working. One even went shopping for an out-of-town crew member who brought a change of clothes but forgot his skivvies.

The mood of workers putting in long hours and performing other job functions than usual was "excellent," said KG&E's Elliott. "People who may have differences of opinion quickly laid those aside," he said.

The regional manager also said the company's crisis management program worked well. "If this had happened 20 years ago, it would have taken three weeks (to restore power)."

The windstorm is not expected to have an immediate effect on KG&E's rates, but "at some point when we go in to develop a rate strategy, this will be taken into account," Elliott said.

Although none had damages comparable to KG&E's, other utility companies also suffered losses be-

cause of the storms.

KPL Gas Service reported less than $1 million in damage from about half a dozen storms. More than 40,000 KPL customers lost their electricity in the June storms.

United Telephone Co. reported 700 customers losing service and between $500,000 and $1 million in damage following the Hesston tornado. Southwestern Bell Telephone had about 4,000 customers who experienced problems after the June windstorm, and damages of $300,000. Rural electric cooperatives also suffered damage.

While many worked overtime tabulating losses, those in the construction industry were burning the candle trying to take care of increasing sales. Hutchinson's Stuckey Lumber was doing triple its usual summer business, mostly selling roofing materials to those making repairs from hail damage, said part-owner Frank Stuckey.

"We've just been working 85, 90 hours a week," he said. "The roofing companies are just going crazy. New companies sprung up overnight."

By the end of August, business had dropped to about double the normal level. "It feels like a vacation," Stuckey said. ☐

1990 Storm Damage Estimated at $150 Million

The tornadoes that swept through central and northeast Kansas caused an estimated $32.7 million damage, according to the state adjutant general's office, which includes the division of emergency preparedness. Harvey County, which had the most damage, had losses of almost $25 million, including about $22 million in Hesston.

Lon Buller, Harvey County emergency preparedness coordinator, said 84 homes were destroyed and 135 sustained major damage in Hesston, and 40 homes were destroyed or damaged in the county. Figures from the Red Cross were even higher: 136 homes destroyed and 84 with major damage.

In Reno County, about 25 homes were damaged or destroyed and 71 outbuildings destroyed, reported emergency preparedness director Bill Walker.

Reno County was pelted again April 9 with a wind and hail storm that caused an estimated $15 million damage, mostly to roofs, Walker said. There was another wind storm June 2, another tornado and hail storm June 7, and a tornado and wind storm also on June 19. Damage for the three months totaled about $25 million.

"In a 90-day period, it was (something) just almost every day," Walker said. "It's brought emergency services together. We're very fortunate that we didn't lose any lives. We were on top of the situation; it was that or it was going to be on top of us."

For a series of storms from May 24 through June 19, state disaster declarations were issued for 16 counties and Gov. Hayden also asked that President George Bush declare the areas as disasters, enabling property owners to apply for federal low-interest loans. The counties listed in the report to Washington were: Barton, Ellsworth, Rice, McPherson and Marion for a May 24 tornado; Wilson, Labette, Neosho and Kingman for flooding at the end of May; Marshall County for wind damage June 7 and Lyon County for a June 7 tornado; and Sedgwick, Harvey, Reno, Rice, Kingman, Grant and Butler for the June 19 windstorm.

The report to the White House — sent through the regional director of the Federal Emergency Management Agency (FEMA) — lists estimates of more than $15 million in damage to farm buildings and machinery and $34 million in crop damage for the May 24 to June 19 period. Some counties did not supply dollar figures of damage. And although crop damage was significant for some individual farmers, agricultural officials said overall damage was much less than that caused by the severe drought of 1989. The report to FEMA also said more than 90 homes, mostly farm homes, were damaged in the 16 counties; at least 240 homes in Sedgwick County were damaged, about 40 of those totally destroyed. About 70 businesses were damaged in Sedgwick County.

Newspaper reports following the June 19 windstorm put preliminary damage estimates as high as $80 million. About half that occurred in Sedgwick County, the majority in rural areas, said Pat Glynn, a disaster management officer for the county. Of the damage, $20 million was attributed to KG&E alone.

Despite the plea for a presidential disaster declaration, FEMA denied Kansas' request. The reason was the small percentage — about 10 percent — of uninsured damage, said Gen. Dan Karr, deputy

'In a 90 day period it was (something) just almost every day.'
— Bill Walker

113

Oklahoma Gas and Electric personnel assist KG&E in the massive task of replacing downed lines and poles following the June 19 inland hurricane. Photo courtesy of KG&E.

'This year was quite a bit more severe.'

— Tim Elliott

director of the Kansas Division of Emergency Preparedness.

"While the storm was very widespread, generally speaking, the damage was covered by insurance," Karr said. "There were some people that didn't have a dime's worth of insurance, but by and large it was a storm system that caused damage that was insured."

Although the presidential declaration was not granted, the U.S. Small Business Administration made declarations of its own which allowed business and personal property owners to apply for low-interest disaster loans.

According to the SBA Area III Disaster Office in Fort Worth, Texas, 31 homeowners and nine businesses applied for SBA disaster loans from the Hesston tornado. In the Sedgwick County area, unofficial totals for the June windstorm were 24 home and personal property loans and five business loans.

Most SBA loans were for uninsured losses and were not included in damage amounts reported by insurance agents. The Independent Insurance Agents of Kansas (IIAK) said in July that nearly $130 million in insured damages were caused by the major spring and summer storms.

IIAK's breakdown of initial estimates of private insurance coverage showed that wind, hail and flood damage was much more than the damage caused by the tornadoes.

Following a July 25 informal survey, the Kansas Insurance Department estimated insured losses at $140 million to $150 million. Some 30,000 automobile claims were expected, the average for $1,300, said Tim Elliott, of the consumer assistance division.

Property claims were expected to number about 50,000, the average for less than $2,000.

"This year was quite a bit more severe, at least so far, compared to other years," Elliott said.

Farm Bureau Mutual Insurance Co. expected that by year's end, 1990 would be the biggest year in dollars and numbers for the 52-year-old company, said claims manager Gary Henton. The company is the largest insurance company in Kansas and has 150 offices in the state.

In 1988, "a superb year," Farm Bureau Mutual had 6,652 claims worth $5.2 million. In 1989, it had more than 11,000 worth $12.6 million but surpassed those totals in just the first seven months of 1990, when it received more than 12,000 claims worth $19 million, Henton said.

For Cimarron Investment Co., the series of severe storms in Kansas and other parts of the Midwest generated significant losses that caused American Fidelity Corp. of Oklahoma City to renegotiate its purchase price for the Cimarron company from between $19 and $20 a share to $11.37 a share.

Because of relatively smaller losses in 1988 and 1989 that allowed companies to build capital and their practice of buying reinsurance, Kansas companies were not adversely affected by the 1990 storms, the insurance department's Elliott said.

"We don't have any indication there's going to be any insolvencies." As for ths storms' effect on rates, Elliott said: "Most people won't see any impact immediately, but eventually it will be filtered into the (loss) experience."

□

The MDS bus arrived in Hesston Tuesday night, hours after the tornado and became the organization's headquarters for the duration of the relief efforts. Photo by Irvin Harms.

Relief and Recovery:

1990 Storms Test Resolve and Reserves of MDS

On March 13, Irvin and Evelyn Harms were returning to Kansas from visiting relatives in Pennsylvania. As they neared the Missouri-Kansas border, the radio reported the probability of storms in central Kansas later that day.

As they neared Emporia, "the sky was plumb clear," recalled Irvin, who is chairman of the Kansas unit of the Mennonite Disaster Service. "I thought, 'There's not going to be a storm. No way.'" But the weather was humid, and a few hours later, what became known as the Hesston tornado began swirling up dirt near Pretty Prairie in south Reno County.

Only a few hours after the Harms had reached their farm south of Moundridge, the first reports of the tornado were broadcast on radio and TV, Irvin called Vernon Miller, a Hutchinson realtor who, as coordinator of MDS for Kansas, handles logistics for the hundreds of volunteers.

Within the hour, Harms and other MDS volunteers headed for Hesston, the same city where MDS had gotten its start 40 years earlier. One carload of volunteers on the way had to take shelter when they encountered the McPherson County tornado just before 7 p.m.

After surveying the damage in Hesston, Harms and several other MDS volunteers drove to Newton to pick up the MDS operations bus, which served as the organization's headquarters during the long cleanup. They then drove the bus back to Hesston.

"When we came into town, there were flashing lights going off all over," said Harms, who serves as the state MDS chairman and has volunteered with the organization for the past 30 years. One of his first relief experiences was after the killer Udall tornado of 1955.

The bus was waved through roadblocks and MDS officials set up headquarters outside the elementary school. With lighting provided by generators, car lights and flashlights, the search through the rubble began. It was not known until the next morning that Hesston had miraculously survived the tornado without a fatality, although two residents of nearby communities were killed.

During the evening, Vernon Miller's wife, Lena, had received calls from MDS volunteers in Virginia, Colorado, Missouri and Winnipeg, Canada, asking if they should send help.

"There was no way we could have utilized all that help," said Harms. "We told them to stay at home."

Harms returned to Moundridge, but after an hour and a half of sleep, he was wakened when the phone began ringing at 5 a.m. Harms headed back to Hesston to find several hundred people waiting for instructions. "It scared you to death to see 400 people waiting for work," Harms said.

There were several hundred MDS volunteers in the city that morning, and the total number of volunteers, members of other relief agencies and law enforcement personnel swelled to more than 2,000.

With patience and serenity as their unspoken bywords, the MDS volunteers went to work in Hesston as they did in towns and on farms along the 120-mile path of the tornado — and as they did at the site of other tornadoes and storms that were to strike Kansas the next few months.

The seal for the organization founded in Hesston 40 years ago.

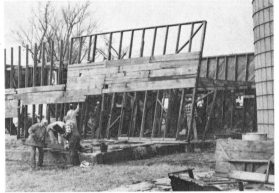

Far Right: Volunteers help collect information from tornado survivors at the Hesston Middle School. Photo by Bob Latta.

Members of Zoar Mennonite Brethren Church help dismantle a barn on the Paul and Rosella Funk farm near Inman. Photo by Jeremy Funk.

> '*I never believed they (volunteers) would come out like they did.*'
>
> — Vernon Miller

Many of those hit by the March 13 tornadoes and in the wind shear storm of June 19 were Mennonites who had helped others in earlier disasters. Now their fellow MDS volunteers were there to lend a helping hand.

Altogether, nearly 1,000 MDS volunteers converged on central Kansas to help with the cleanup in the Hesston, Pretty Prairie, Haven, Yoder, Burrton, Goessel, Hillsboro, Dwight and Inman areas.

Vernon Miller concentrated on coordinating the relief efforts in the Yoder-Haven area. Not only were farmers faced with rebuilding their homes, barns and outbuildings, but with restoring their fields as well. "Sometimes it takes days to go through the fields and clear it of debris," Miller said.

Even months later, MDS was still at work. There was long-range relief and rebuilding to take care of, and sometimes that included trying to boost the spirits of the victims.

Harold Voth, the husband of Ruth Voth, who was killed when the tornado struck their farm near Goessel, did not know if he wanted to rebuild on the site and initially refused to take a donation from MDS.

"He returned our initial check," Harms said. "I went to talk with him a long time, and he finally decided to take it." Voth decided that rather than move away, he wanted to live on the land that he and his wife had shared, and moved into a mobile home on the site. He discussed with MDS plans to build a new house in late August. On September 15, 1990, six months after the tornado took his wife's life, Harold Voth died of cancer.

The MDS volunteers are trained to listen and offer spiritual support up to a point, Harms said. But sometimes the survivors break down, "and you have to go and get a pastor to talk to them," Harms said.

Tornadoes continued unmercifully the next two months, and MDS was there. Before the March 13 storm, Kansas MDS volunteers had not been called to a large-scale disaster in their home state in several years.

"We had some minor things to keep up interest," said Miller. "We had a question on whether or not we could get people to respond if it (a disaster) were here. I never believed they would come out like they did."

The June 19 wind shear storm that swept through parts of Kingman, Reno, Sedgwick and Harvey counties struck at much of the heart of Mennonite country in central Kansas.

"By the time of the June 19 storm," Harms recalled, "we were almost burned out and we had our harvest work to do. A lot of repairs had to be postponed." By late August, the MDS volunteers began to catch up with requests for rebuilding assistance.

Throughout their history, the Mennonite and Amish communities have helped neighbors in need by doing everything from household and farm chores to rebuilding homes and barns.

Through MDS, that helping tradition has taken on a national and international scope. MDS volunteers from Mennonite, Amish and Brethren in Christ churches in the United States and Canada have rallied to help the victims of floods, tornadoes and hurricanes dig out

Many people were helped by M.D.S..
Established in Kansas
Nos how to take care of people.
Nos how to help people.
On location when the tornado hit.
Nos about tornados.
It raises funds.
There tornado helpers
Established in Hesston

Disaster service.
Intails M.D.S.
Services are voluntary
Another helper for disasters
Supplies people
There mennonite
Evergoneneeds help from M.D.S. who shurt
Ready for disasters.

Stationed around the U.S.
everyone enjoys them.
ready to serve people
Varies from place to place
In the U.S. only
Cares about people
Everywhere a disaster is

Jason Martin
Trisha Martin

How do you spell relief? Jason Martin and Trisha Martin spell it MENNONITE DISASTER SERVICE in their writing. The Hesston seventh graders express their thoughts in this verse for their seventh grade class project.

from under the rubble and begin to rebuild their lives.

The scale of today's Mennonite Disaster Services is a sharp contrast to the organization's humble beginnings four decades ago in Kansas.

In the summer of 1950, a group of young Mennonites from the Pennsylvania (now Whitestone) Mennonite Church in Hesston, decided to form a disaster relief organization. As conscientious objectors during World War II, the men worked in the Civilian Public Service.

Inspired by their work in hospitals and overseas missions, the men wanted to keep their volunteer spirit alive. Working under the motto, "Bear ye one another's burdens, and so fulfill the law of Christ," the group began offering their help in emergencies. First the group went to emergencies in Kansas, then throughout the region.

The idea of a congregation-based relief organization caught on and other Mennonite congregations joined in. In 1961, MDS became a part of the Akron, Penn.-based Mennonite Central Committee, a nationwide volunteer network.

Because the string of tornadoes on March 13 had struck in many Mennonite communities, MDS coordinators did not have to call up volunteers from local congregations. Instead, the volunteers began driving around checking on neighbors.

Ray and Irma Siemens were helped by MDS volunteers just after their home six miles west of Inman was destroyed by a funnel cloud, less than two hours after the Hesston tornado. The Siemens were walking along

the road looking for help when a carload of MDS volunteers picked them up. The group was on its way back from Hesston, when they spotted the Siemens.

Nearly 50 MDS workers and other neighbors were back the next morning to help the Siemens clear away the rubble that had been their home. Volunteers lifted the house's fallen walls to search for belongings and help clear away the debris.

"They gathered up what they could," Irma said. "I had to laugh when I was unpacking. At the bottom of one box, someone had saved me one leg of a chair. I saved it, too. Someone was thinking of me."

As members of the Mennonite Church, the Siemens had participated in MDS relief projects before, but Irma Siemens said she was surprised at the group's cooperative spirit and size. "I never thought there would be so many to come out," she said.

Armed with chainsaws, rakes, heavy equipment and their bare hands, MDS volunteers began to cut away fallen trees and clear debris. Later they would concentrate on helping with repairs.

Melvin Miller, state MDS secretary, was one of the volunteers who went out on the cleanup after the March 19 storm, the Claflin tornado and the June 19 windstorm. A sewing machine salesman and repairman by trade, Miller, like many other MDS volunteers, dropped his work to help.

What motivates this quiet and unassuming group of volunteers? Melvin Miller spoke softly as he answered the question. There is a lot of satisfaction "in helping someone," he said. "When you see the way people

Evelyn and Irvin Harms, Moundridge. Irvin is Kansas Unit Mennonite Disaster Service chairman.

'It scared you to death to see 400 people waiting for work.'

— Irvin Harms

Dillons gave food and water
Everybody helped clean up
Volunteers offered their time
Air force
Schools gave shelter
Tabor college
An Elementary class helped clean up
The M.DS
I helped clean up
Outsiders
News, newpapers and friends

By Melinda Redger
& Gretchen Rhodes

Cleanup after a tornado means careful attention to sifting through the debris for valued possessions, as seen in this photo of volunteers in Hesston by Bob Latta.

DEVASTATION was written by Melinda Redger and Gretchen Rhodes in their 7th grade class in Hesston.

respond, the emotions can get to you."

Pressed to explain the MDS commitment, Miller said, "It's part of our Mennonite culture. We don't have a monopoly on compassion. We're just better organized."

MDS is based on a network of 3,000 Mennonite, Amish and Brethren in Christ congregations in the United States and Canada. Each congregation is encouraged to take care of small emergencies that may come up in its area. When the disaster is too large, MDS coordinators are contacted to call in help from other areas. If that is not enough, help can be mobilized on a nationwide scale.

While MDS does accept donations for supplies and expenses, its efforts are focused on augmenting the efforts of other relief organizations. "Without the Red Cross and the Salvation Army, we couldn't operate," said Harms. "They furnish food and lodging."

Without the help of the MDS, David Wesseler said his family would have spent months, perhaps years, wading through the rubble of their farm near Lorraine.

Wesseler's farm was one of many near Claflin, Bushton and Lorraine to be damaged or destroyed by the May 24 tornadoes.

About 230 MDS workers spent three days cleaning up what was left of the Wesseler farm. The tornado destroyed nearly everything, including the house, a mobile home, the granary and barn.

One of the things MDS volunteers are trained to keep in mind is that people are more important than things. Often, disaster victims are in shock and don't

'When you see the way people respond, the emotions can get to you.'

— Melvin Miller

know what they want to save from the rubble, said Homer Wedel, MDS state treasurer.

The MDS approach is to sift through the debris and leave the decision on what is valuable to the victims, Wedel said.

A rural Moundridge seed dealer and semi-retired farmer, Wedel has gone on MDS relief efforts for the past 40 years. Wedel was one of the MDS volunteers who traveled to Wichita Falls, Texas, in 1975 to help clean up after a tornado hit that city.

In past years, Wedel said, volunteering for MDS had been a strain on his farm operation and seed business. But during the several weeks he spent in Hesston, his customers understood, he said.

After the Claflin tornado, MDS volunteers mobilized twice more. Sixty volunteers traveled to Emporia for a day's worth of cleanup after a tornado hit the city on June 7. Less than two weeks later, volunteers would be called again from throughout central Kansas to help clean up after a tornadic force wind storm rushed through several central Kansas counties June 19.

At the farm of Lynn and Kathy Geffert north of Haven, 50 MDS volunteers spent an afternoon building pasture fence. The half-mile of five-strand barbed wire took the group about six hours to put up. "It's the straightest fence I've ever seen," said Kathy Geffert.

The work of the men and women of the Mennonite Disaster Service in 1990 — whether it was building fences, rebuilding houses or helping to rebuild lives — more than lived up to the proud tradition that began 40 years ago in the heart of central Kansas. □

Survivors of the March 13 Tornadoes

Editor's Note: The following is a list of individuals, families and businesses whose property was damaged by the tornadoes of March 13. The primary source material was provided by officials of the counties affected and supplemented by our research.

Although we made every effort to be comprehensive, the list may not include everyone. But we believe this list is nonetheless an important historical record and that it will give readers a sense of the scope of damage that a tornadic storm can produce.

HESSTON

Achilles, Karen
Achilles, Michael
Adkisson, Dean & Betty
Alliman, Kirk & Jean
Andres, Dennis
Arellano, Juanita
Arnold, George & Janice
Bachman, Weldon & Arlene
Balzer, Harlin & Susan
Bandy, Murray & Bessie
Bassinger, Leonard
Beck, Harold & Ruth
Beitler, Bob & Dorie
Bieker, David & Nadine
Birch, Lee & Carol
Bitikofer, Clifford & Elizabeth
Bitikofer, Henry & Luella
Boettger, Conrad & Beth
Boggs, Tom & Barbara
Bontrager, Ivan & Bertha
Boyer, Carl & Joan
Bretz, Ronald & Dorothy
Briar, Stanley & Cindy
Brock, Ron & Ann
Buller, Erby & Esther
Burgess, Don
Buscher, Margo
Buss, Michael & Cathy
Carlisle, Stanley & Imogene
Chaple, Alberto & Maria
Chastain, Jim
Church, Sheryl
Crocker, Boyd
Crocker, Mike & Debbie
Davis, Charles & Cheryl
Davis, Robert & Carol
Day, Dean & Maria

Debardelaben, James C.
Delta & Pineland
DeWitt, Edward & Judy
Dieker, Eddie & Judy
Diener, Dr. Clayton & Inez
Diller, Robert & Marcella
Don Gehring, Photography
Dreier, Velma
Ediger, Bill & Jerilyn
Elementary School
Ensz, Albert & Bertina
Flaming, Warren & Cheryl
Friesen, Paul & Frieda
Fulk, Loren & Ann
Fuller, David & Jeanie
Fuqua, Larry
Gamber, Ruth
Gardner, Scott
Garrett, Robert & Linda
Gingerich, Fred & Alice
Gingerich, Ken & Leona
Good, Lowell & Lena
Good, Robert & Twila
Guengerich, Ronald & Ruth
Hackenberg, Ray & Eleanor
Hair Designs
Hamiiton, Virginia
Hanson, Barbara
Hawkey, Delbert & Darlene
Heidebrecht, Ernie & Marie
Henderson, Eric
Heritage Inn
Hesston Auto & Truck
Hesston Builders
Hesston College
Hesston Colonial House
Hesston Concrete

Hesston Decorating Center
Hesston Electric
Hesston Insurance
Hesston Machine & Welding
Hesston Post Office
Hesston State Bank
Hesston Veterinary Clinic
Hogsett, Chester & Yvonne
Hoheisel, Dennis & Jeannine
Holmes, Richard & Wilma
Holsinger, Justus & Salome
Hostetler, Doris
Hostetler, Keith
Hugie, William & Nancy
Hull, Robert & Judy
H.S. Bank
Isaacs, Al
Jantz, Harvey & Alice
Jantz, Roger & Carolyn
Janzen, Richard & Charlene
Janzen, Eldon & Caroline
Janzen, Floyd & Anna Mae
Janzen, Junior & Joyce
Janzen, Leon & Juanita
Janzen, Mrs. Irma
Jost, Lynn & Donna
Karnes, Art & Sonia
Kauffman, Joel & Carol
Kauffman, Clara
Keim, Howard & Tammy
King, Alberta
King Construction
Kluver, Donald
Koehn, Gilbert & Irene
Krehbiel, Kerry & Nancy
Krehbiel, Rollins & Louise
Kremer, Lorne & Hazel

Kropf Lumber
Lais, Larry & Thelma
Latta, Robert & Loretta
Leinbach, Gerald & Lois
Lichti, Leonard & Pearl
Lichti, Tom & Janice
Livengood, Kenneth & Gale
Loebsack, Victor & Margo
Malm, Steve
Martins, Melvin & Mildred
Matz, Kirk & Debbie
McElmurry, Elsie
McKinley, John
Miles, Conrad & Priscilla
Miller, Dawna
Miller, Milton & Lorraine
Mininger, Collette
Moland, George & Sally
Morris, Richard & Janice
Nebel, Brian & Beth
Neufeld, James
Nickell, Merle & Valerie
Niemczyk, Samuel
Nikkel, Gene & Carol
Nilsen, Lana
Old Fina Station
Ole Town Cleaners
Osborne, Chester & Eva
O'Halloran, Michael & Beth
Patterson, Dean & Sandy
Pauls, Gary & Debi
Pauls, Inc
Peirce, Ray & Carol
Peters, Lelyn & Jessie
Pfautz, Alma
Pizza Hut
Pohlenz, Richard & Sheryl

Continued from Page 119

Price, Gary & Rosilind
Pruitt, Martin & Sharon
Quiring, Cheryl
Randolph, Robert & Julia
Ratzlaff, Bette
Regier, James & Mary Ann
Regier, Mrs. Herbert
Regier, John
Reif, Sharon
Reimer, Irvin & Edna
Reimer, James & Dorothy
Reimer Plbg & Htg
Reimer, Robert & Geneva
Rempel, Scott & Brenda
Robinson, Lynn
Rogers, Kent & Sondra
Roth, Dwight & Lynette
Roupp, Milford & Rosie
Roupp, Willard & Elda
Rupp, Wilson
Saltzman, Erna
Sanborn, Dan & Andrea
Save-A-Trip
Sawin, Tom & Ruby
Saylor, Richard & Jan
Schmidt, Eldon & Luella
Schmidt, Junia & Doris
Schmidt, Ruth
Schmucker, Marjorie
Schrag, Lee
Schroeder, Keith & Nancy
Schwanke, Kendall & Judy
Sebits, David & Dixie
Sherwood, Ross
Shoemaker, Orval & Verna
Sieber, Richard & Annie
Simpson, Dallas & Carolyn
Snyder, John & Nona
Staley, Larry
Stallings, Phil
Stauffer, Randy & Pat
Stauffer, Roger & Claridy
Stehman, Glenn & Joanne
Stratton, Verna
Suderman, Dianne
Sunglo Feeds
The Source (Hesston Electric)
Troyer Furniture--(D&P)
Troyer, Jake & Anna Joy
Troyer, Jerry & Wilma
U-Do-It Car Wash
Uhrig, Verlyn & Sandy
Voran, Willis & Amanda

Voth, Alfred & Clara
Voth, Charley & Lillian
Voth, Waldo & Orpha
Warders, Tom & Lois
Weaver, Bob & Phyllis
Weaver, Don & Pam
Weber, Robert & Linda
Wedel, Delbert & Carol
Welton, Roy & Reita
Wenger, Richard & Chris
West, Don
Wiens, Ernst & Margy
Wiens, Richard & Mary Lou
Wiggers, Earl & Louise
Willems, LuAlan & Judy
Wise-Martin, Vincent & Rachel
Yoder, Arlan & Ila
Yoder, Gene & Dorothy
Yoder, James & Phyllis
Yoder, Melvin & Cleo
Ziegler, Joe & Nadine
Zielke, John & Jude
Zook, Lloyd & Loretta
Zook, Marvin & Dorothy

GEARY COUNTY
Mayer, Hal

HARVEY COUNTY RURAL
Baumann, Allen & Sharon
Bayless, Steve & Vicki
Berger, Stanley
Bontrager, Eli & Opal
Burkett, David
Clark, E. C.
Corcoran, G. A.
Devenpeck, John
Fisher, Kent & Dixie
Flickinger, Jake, Sr.
Flickinger, Larry
Friesen, Robert
Friesen, Robert & Virginia
Goering, Milo
Graber, Marlo
Hasty, Leona
Holdeman, Clinton
Holdeman, Kenneth
Koehn, Art
Koehn, Edward
Krehbiel, Kim
Leatherman, Dean & Sandra
Martin, Luke
Mitchell, Cecil
Monroe, George

Moyer, Jim
Owens, William
Plenert, Jerry
Regier, Reinhard
Reubke, John
Spragg, Larry
Stucky, Kenneth
Swartzendruber, Stan & Sharon
Toews, Bill & Annie
Troxel, Clarence
Unruh, Gary
Unruh, Lowell
Vogt, Arnold
Vogt, Weldon
Wedel, Paul
Wiens, Dale
Wiens, Henry

MARION COUNTY
Ag. Service Inc.
Bina, Ernest & Agnes
Buller, Jon & Shelley
Flaming, Dennis
Flaming, Dwight
Flaming, Edward & Shirley
Friesen, Dennis R. & CleoBeth
Funk, LeRoy & Alice
Haefner, Mary
Klaasen, Donald
Klassen, Carl & Betty
Lueker, Laverne
Neuwirth, Robert & Rose Mary
Pankratz, H. D.
Pritz, Selma
Ratzlaff, Isaac
Regier, Allan
Regier, Jack & Evelyn
Rindt, Lawrence
Rudolph, Daniel
Schmidt, Fred & JoAnn
Schmidt, James & Diana
Schmidt, Randy & Meribeth
Thiessen, James & Joyce
Thiessen, Linden & Doreen
Voth, Harold
Wiens, ElRoy & Loretta

McPHERSON COUNTY
Dick, Russell
Froese, Don
Funk, Paul & Rosella
Gillmore, Bret & Marla
Koehn, Sidney
Neufeldt, Kelvin & Em

Nikkel, Leland
Schmidt, Arlo
Schroeder, Alvie
Seiler, Fred & Jan
Siemens, Ray & Irma
Stucky, Elfriede
Thiessen, John and Jan
Zerger, Dick

MORRIS COUNTY
Brown, Max
Cronin, John & Laura
Monnich, Warner
Oleen, Arden
Oleen, Jan & Lo Jean
Shelton, Donald

RENO COUNTY
Ark Valley Electric
Astle, Mick & Edna
Astle, Robert
Beltz, Quinlin
Berndsen, Henry & Eileen
Bontrager, Dave
Brauer, Tony & Connie
Doerksen, Harold J.
Dwyer, Dick & Margaret
Edgington, John
Foreman, Lee
Fry, Floyd & Polly
Geffert, Bill
Geffert, Lynn & Cathy
Haines, Carolyn
Johnson, Carl
Kincaid, Russell
Lafond, Joe
Meier, Delmar
Pitts Oil Product
Pleasant Grove Church
Popp, Hal
Rogers, Bill
Royer, Bill & Leta
Snodgrass, David
Stade, Milton
Stalcup, Harold
Webster, Floyd
Yoder, Thomas J.
Yoder, Toby & Wilma

WABAUNSEE COUNTY
Bellinger, Jim
Meseke, Robert
O'Neill, Glenn
Sylvester, Elgene